# An Expert Look at Love, Intimacy and Personal Growth

# An Expert Look at Love, Intimacy and Personal Growth

## Selected Papers in Psychoanalytic Social Psychology

### Second Edition

Robert M. Gordon, Ph.D.

Dedicated to Benjamin D. Gordon

# Related books by Robert M. Gordon:

*I Love You Madly! On Passion, Personality and Personal Growth* (2006, 2008)

*I Love You Madly! Workbook: Insight Enhancement about Healthy and Disturbed Love Relations* (2007)

ISBN 978-0-9779616-5-8
Library of Congress Control Number 2007942193

IAPT Press, 1259 S. Cedar Crest Blvd., Suite 325, Allentown, PA 18103 For extra copies: www.mmpi-info.com, online bookstores, www.atlasbooks.com, or call 800-247-6553.

# Acknowledgments

I would like to thank Alla Gordon for her help in editing, and the original publishers for permission to reprint the material for this book. I rewrote and summarized most of the material.

Adopted with permission from *Psychology Today:* Horn, J. (1976). "Love: The Most Important Ingredient in Happiness." *Psychology Today, 10*(2), 98–102 (a summary of dissertation by R. M. Gordon).

Adopted with permission from Brunner/Mazel: Gordon, R. M. (1982). "Systems-Object Relations View of Marital Therapy: Revenge and Reraising." In L. R. Wolberg, & M. Aronson (Eds.), *Group and Family Therapy.* London: Brunner-Mazel.

Adopted with permission from *Security Management,* and with permission of Debra Kay Woolever Bennett: "How to Pick a Good Apple," by Debra Kay Woolever Bennett, and Robert M. Gordon, *Security Management* (1986), 101–103.

Adopted with permission, this is an edited version of Gordon, R. M. (1993) "Ethics Based on Protection of the Transference," which first appeared in *Issues in Psychoanalytic Psychology, 15*(2), 95–105.

Adopted with permission, this is an edited version of Gordon, R. M. (1995b). "The Symbolic Nature of the Supervisory Relationship: Identification and Professional Growth," which first appeared in *Issues in Psychoanalytic Psychology 17*(2), 154–162.

Adopted with permission, this is an edited version of Gordon, R. M. (2001) "MMPI/MMPI-2 Changes in Long-Term Psychoanalytic Psychotherapy," which first appeared in *Issues in Psychoanalytic Psychology, 23,* (1 and 2), 59–79.

Death" (1999), and "Judge Psychology by Results and Scientific Studies" (2005), both by Robert M. Gordon.

Adopted with permission, Gordon, R. M. (2006e). "What Is Love? A Unified Model of Love Relations," first appeared in *Issues in Psychoanalytic Psychology, 28*(1), 25–33.

Adopted with permission, Gordon, R. M., Stoffey, R., & Bottinelli, J. (in press, 2008). "MMPI-2 Findings of Primitive Defenses in Alienating Parents," *American Journal of Family Therapy.*

# Table of Contents

# Introduction

From over a span of 30 years, I studied and treated disturbances of personality and intimacy with the expert's tools of:

1. Case study,
2. Empirical research, and
3. Theoretical formulation.

I will tell you what I have learned about the nature of love, healthy and unhealthy intimacy and how to bring about personal growth. For this purpose, I rewrote and summarized some of my published papers. I picked the most relevant and made them accessible for the student and intelligent layperson. Much of the problems that people have are interpersonal in nature (social psychological) and from unconscious factors (psychoanalytic). This is why I call this collection of writings *psychoanalytic social psychology.*

In college, my main interest was science, particularly theory building. I was curious about how scientists develop theories. Wondering how we come to understand and explain things (epistemology) led me to psychology, the science of the brain and mind.

As an undergraduate, I coauthored research on preventive mental health with children, research on how people might have personal growth in groups, and research on defense mechanisms. I learned that the idea of change seemed easy, but defense mechanisms made change very difficult.

I learned how we form our own naive psychological theories. We rarely correct and update our personal theories of others and ourselves. We often bring our biases into our intimacies. We tend to remain defensive about our thinking even if it repeatedly leads to dysfunction.

Despite their best intentions, even scientists bring their biases into their research. In my second year of the Ph.D. program in psychology, I did a study that showed how researchers could produce biased findings. I found that I could manipulate a person's perceived effectiveness of a treatment. I gave all the subjects the same treatment for anxiety, i.e., progressive relaxation.

People rated the treatment valuable or not, based largely on how I recruited the subjects. **"Effects of Volunteering and Responsibility on the Perceived Value and Effectiveness of a Clinical Treatment"** was published in the *Journal of Consulting and Clinical Psychology* in 1976.

I demonstrated in my study that one could get the desired results based on the motivations of volunteer subjects and using obvious self-reports about the treatment.

Today there are too many biased studies "proving" the effectiveness of short-term superficial treatments. They have problems of poor external validity (real-life applications). Most people have symptoms because of their personality traits. Personality traits do not easily change with low-dose treatments.

In contrast, in 2001, I published research on treatment effectiveness. This time it was with patients with strong defenses, resistances, and with long-standing complex problems. The treatment dose was high with long-term psychoanalytic psychotherapy. The treatment was aimed at disturbed personality traits. The outcome measure was not an obvious self-report, but a standardized psychological test (MMPI, Minnesota Multiphasic Personality Inventory) that measures enduring personality traits. I wanted to measure personal growth in high-dose psychotherapy. (I will share my findings in chapter 7.)

If our theories of life are biased, there is dysfunction. This is true for all belief systems. This is true for people's biased view of themselves and others. This is true for scientific research. So let us begin to see how a scientist-practitioner can try to understand the problems of love, intimacy, and personal growth.

# Chapter 1 Love and Happiness

For my Ph.D. dissertation, I explored what made people happy and why. My dissertation involved 13 experiments including developing my own test of values (the REVIR test). I looked at both economic and interpersonal resources and how their exchange affected one's quality of life.

In 1976, *Psychology Today* (J. Horn) reviewed my Ph.D. dissertation, ***Effects of Interpersonal and Economic Resources upon Values and the Quality of Life*** (1975), in their article "Love: The Most Important Ingredient in Happiness."

I took a look at some of the main causes of happiness. I used Uriel G. Foa's resource-exchange theory. Foa (1974) brilliantly brought together psychological theory and economic theory into a single model. He theorized that the mind classified exchangeable resources into categories.

According to Foa, people exchange six main resources in their relations with others: **love** (warmth, affection), **status** (respect, esteem), **information** (advice, knowledge), **money, goods, and services** (work, labor).

The main psychological resources that we can exchange are: love, status, and information. The main economic resources that we can exchange are money, goods, and services.

Love and money are resources at opposite ends of the particular–universal dimension. Love is the most particularistic resource. We exchange it with only a few carefully chosen people. Money on the other hand, is universal; we exchange it with nearly anyone.

There is also the symbolic–concrete dimension. Status and information are resources that are more symbolic and goods and services are resources that are more concrete. Foa developed a mathematical circumplex of psychological and economic resources along these two dimensions (see Figure 1.1).

Resources at opposite ends of dimensions are less similar in a person's mind, and therefore less substitutable than resources next to one another. For example, money and information are next to one another. The credit card is between money and information. A credit card has elements of both having monetary and information value.

However, money is at the opposite end of love and is not a good substitute resource for love. Services are a more acceptable substitute for love. For example, some parents can only concretely show love through giving services (care giving).

In my dissertation research, I developed tests to measure how much value a person placed on each resource, how much of each resource a

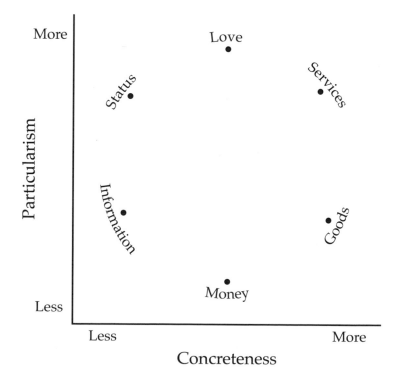

Figure 1.1   Foa's model of psychological and economic resources along a mathematical circumplex.

person had received as a child, how much a person was receiving presently, and how happy the person was.

The REVIR (Relative Exchange Value of Interpersonal Resources) test measures the value individuals assign to each of the six resources Foa described, plus sex. Sex is a resource between love and services on Foa's mathematical circumplex. It can be closer to either love or services depending on the degree of intimacy.

The REVIR test consists of 63 questions in three elements of life: work, marriage, and wish. The type of work individuals would like to do and the kind of spouse they prefer reflects values. I included questions on wishes to let people express their values if social institutions did not constrain them.

The questions offer a series of choices among the seven resources. In the portion of the test devoted to wishes, for example, each question starts out: "If I had my choice between two wishes, I would prefer . . ." Then there are 21 either/or choices, such as: "(a) to have financial security or (b) to have great knowledge and wisdom . . . (a) to have a life of wealth and luxury or (b) to have a fulfilling sex life." By the time someone answers all the questions, he or she will have ranked money, love and five other resources 21 different times.

Similar choices are presented in the 21 spouse questions and the 21 work questions. By adding the number of times a person preferred each resource in the 63 choices, I came up with a score that reflects how important each resource is to an individual.

To uncover the personal history behind these preferences, I developed a Resource Income Survey (RIS) to identify which resources individuals had received most in childhood, which they are receiving currently, and how happy they are.

I had to validate my tests. In doing so, I found that I had to make corrections to an early version of the RIS based on the preliminary results.

I got lopsided results to the question, "How much love did you receive as a child?" Most people claimed that they received a lot of love. (Later I found in my clinical work that people have trouble perceiving how much they were loved.) When I changed the question on my test to, "How demonstrative was your mother in showing love?"—I received more varied responses.

I administered the REVIR and RIS tests to 346 students. The full and part-time day and evening students at Temple University provided a wide range of age, ethnicity, and economic backgrounds.

I found that love correlated most closely with happiness, followed by the two other particularistic resources, services and status.

How much any one resource affects happiness depended partly on how well it worked with other resources in contributing to a person's happiness. For example, I found that much of the happiness derived from sex results from its association with love.

I found that love was responsible for three quarters of the effect all resources had on the students' happiness, with services, feeling financially secure, sex and information accounting for the rest. Beyond that, additional money, status, and goods have no real effect on happiness.

Poverty brings suffering that only money can cure. However, after people are living within their means and paying their bills, additional riches have little lasting effect on enduring happiness. It seems that well-off people eventually habituate to their wealth. The riches are too different a resource to compensate for any problems with intimacy.

I found little relationship between people's family incomes when they were a child and how much they valued money as adults. However, the amount of love an individual received in childhood had a strong effect on the current valuation of both love and money.

If the students received little love as children, by adulthood they defensively learned to devalue love as a reliable resource. Those who came from families in which love and money were both scarce placed the least value on love.

Students who grew up in love-poor families valued money much more than those who received a lot of love as children. This was true whether their families were poor or were well off.

It seems that when money is scarce, people learn to concentrate their energies on financial survival. Students from affluent but love-poor families, on the other hand, may learn to value money as a substitute for love, as a means of security, or as an indication of their personal worth.

I found that adults who felt they were not receiving much love currently, usually overvalued goods as a resource. It was as if they felt that they would get more immediate gratification from the possession of an object than from an intimacy, which they grew to associate with frustration.

If this materialism is an attempt to compensate for a lack of love, it is not likely to work. People who placed a high value on money and goods tended to avoid the intimate commitments that are most likely to give them the love that they need. It is also important to distinguish between the use of things as substitutes for relationships versus the healthy enjoyment of the finer things in life. The rejection of money and materialism does not make one noble or loveable. The point is that no amount of money or goods can substitute for the happiness that comes from a healthy love relationship.

Money or goods were the most common substitutes for love, but some people use information (ideas) instead. The overintellectualized individual may find it easier to manipulate ideas than to deal with emotions and intimacy.

My research showed that love is by far the most important resource in people's lives. It relates most to happiness. Love plays the biggest role in forming values that guide life choices and lifestyles. The data supports the importance of childhood experiences in the quality of life. Someone who experiences a shortage of love in childhood is likely to have unhappiness as an adult, and might develop beliefs and defenses that perpetuate the unhappiness. How then do we treat this cycle of unhappiness based on childhood traumas with intimacy?

# Chapter 2 Treating Love Disturbances

**"Systems-Object Relations View of Marital Therapy: Revenge and Re-Raising"** was my chapter in the 1982 book, *Group and Family Therapy*. It was a required paper as part of my psychoanalytic training at the Post Graduate Center for Mental Health in New York City. I was interested in theory building. A layperson might think that a *fact* is worth more than a theory. This is not so in science. In science there are no facts, but findings and theories. A good theory organizes findings into a useful big picture. With further research, former "facts" may become errors, and a better theory emerges. Theories that explain and predict are the ultimate aim of science.

I was interested in integrating two theories, family systems theory and object relations theory. Family systems theory helps us understand the interaction between people. Object relations theory helps us understand what is going on inside a person. I felt this combination would provide me with a better way to help people with intimacy disturbances.

The family is a social system that runs on implicit rules. When the boundaries, roles, alliances, and how things are done in the system are dysfunctional, it affects the intrapsychic (internal emotional) system within the developing child.

The family system is also the result of the interacting personalities of its members. The family system and intrapsychic system of the members regulate one another. The therapist can intervene at the level (family or intrapsychic) based on the patient's accessibility and not the therapist's theoretical preference.

Concrete and defensive people might not be able to self-reflect enough to work deeply on their intrapsychic conflicts. Therefore, intervening in the family system might help even defensive individuals be less symptomatic.

I found in my dissertation research that love brought the greatest happiness. If people did not have enough love in childhood, they later were self-defeating in getting the love they needed. Why does that problem continue, and what could be done about it?

I found in that the psychoanalytic area of object relations, people unconsciously repeat their past attachments for better or worse. People tend to regress in intimacy and express attachment issues and conflicts from childhood. We have the choice to unconsciously repeat the past or learn from it and break self-defeating patterns.

Lewis Wolberg wrote in the editors' summary of my chapter:

The author discusses how a combined systems and object relations approach can provide valuable insights into many marital interactions. Since intrapsychic and interpersonal systems are isomorphically related, interventions at one level can often effect changes in others. Systems theory is useful in conceptualizing short-term therapy aimed primarily at symptom relief and for those individuals who are not generally responsive to insight; object relations theory is more pertinent for conceptualizing interpretive interventions. Interpreting distortions of the spouses in terms of their original family situations, as well as in vivo confrontations with their original families, can help to detoxify dysfunctional marital relationships.

A committed intimacy activates unconscious conflicts. It also presents an opportunity for working out these conflicts. Tremendous energy is detonated in the process. Individuals may use a variety of intrapsychic mechanisms to regulate the degree of tension they can tolerate. Higher-level defenses such as humor, sublimation, and suppression help intimacy. Primitive defenses (denial, projection, projective identification, splitting, etc.) hurt intimacy.

The degree of structural maturity of a person determines the amount of tolerance one has—that is, the differentiation and integration of ego-states (parts of personality). When the ego-states work together, there is less intrapsychic conflict.

Likewise, a social system can tolerate tensions based on its degree of differentiation and integration of its members. Systems that are inflexible and maladaptive have primitive defenses (acting out, scapegoating, etc.).

Since the system is more than the summation of its parts, a systems therapist observes how the system as a whole deals with tensions created by changes in membership, boundaries, communication patterns, roles, power, and alliances.

I look at the structural integrity of units (ego-states within personality and the individuals in a family). This structural integrity can go from a healthy integrated complexity to a chaotic and rigid system in both the person and the family.

A major theoretical question has been the locus of pathology and the level of intervention. Pragmatically, this would lead to the issue of where the intervention should then be aimed—at the individual or the family system.

I feel that psychopathology is best represented as a continuous process of interacting units from intrapsychic to social realms isomorphically linked to one another.

Each system must eventually adapt to the other; therefore, an intervention at one level can affect changes at another. I feel that a continuous model allows for interventions at either the intrapsychic or the social level, depending on the most accessible level of intervention.

Some people work very well with insights. They are able to evolve their view of themselves and others. They can use insights to become more objective and have less of the distortions that hurt intimacy (transference of the bad object and projection of the bad self). It is possible to use these insights for personal growth.

For others, insight is not as effective. However, changing the external structure in which they are embedded can have an effect of symptom relief.

In systems thinking, a symptom can provide a homeostatic function. A person's symptom may be seen as a role function necessary for systems operations. If the system changes in a way that no longer requires that role, the symptom may vanish. The therapist may wonder, "Why does it make sense for this person to have this symptom at this time? What is its function for the current social system as well as the intrapsychic system?"

In thinking in terms of social systems, the therapist would ask, "How can this symptom be substituted with something that is less costly and still maintain the operations of the system?"

A symptom can function as an attempt to regulate the degree of tension in an interpersonal system. A symptom can be used to escalate or de-escalate tensions. Examples are:

1. Triangulating someone into the marital dyad, such as original family, friends, lovers, or children,
2. A "sick" or "bad" child becoming the focus of attention, diverting the issue from marital tensions,
3. A "sick" or "bad" spouse becoming the symptom bearer for the marriage, and
4. Distancing by excessive working and obsessional diversions.

These symptomatic sets can be used to create distance and diffusion in order to cool down the relationship. These same symptomatic sets can also be used to escalate the tensions. Although a third party can act as a support and a stabilizing influence in a marriage, the presentation of an interfering parent or lover can create an immediate threat to the same system.

A "sick" or "bad" person may defocus the marital problems, but may eventually tax the emotional resources of the martial system. Obsessional working and diversions may be used to create a tolerable distance from a difficult spouse. However, this may eventually provoke the avoided spouse to pursue more and create more problems.

A person in the pursuing role may fall in love with someone who is enacting a distancing role, precisely since it is safe to pursue an individual knowing that he or she will create a needed distance.

The pursuing spouse may be secretly longing to conquer the rejecting parent, while the distancing spouse may be reassured in his or her ability to escape the impinging, absorbing mother.

These roles may flip-flop back and forth, with both spouses unconsciously colluding to regulate the degree of tolerable intimacy. Regardless of what people consciously state that they want, the degree of tolerable intimacy was set in childhood. It was set in the interaction of the original family system along with the person's innate temperament.

For example, individuals with borderline (immature) personality structures may demand intimacy, but they will unconsciously drive others away with their insatiable demands. Narcissistic personalities may demand intimacy for exploitive needs, but feel entitled to not reciprocate.

Children with normal temperaments, but who were embedded in cold families may later long for closeness, but find ways to be self-defeating and unconsciously repeat their unhappy childhood.

Rigid systems defend against change, but change is inevitable. Change can come when a strong spouse gets sick, or a child grows up and leaves home. An insecure spouse can grow and become more independent.

A sudden shift in roles often releases a great deal of tension, which can bring the system into crisis. The therapist working at the level of the system can use the crisis to help the system become more flexible and adaptive.

The system's structure may vary in its:

1. Degree of permeability or rigidity of the boundaries; i.e., how emotionally accessible are the parents to the children?

2. Differentiation versus enmeshment, i.e., how much independence is allowed?
3. Degree of stability, i.e., the degree of commitment and identification of members with each other, and
4. Alignments or alliances, i.e., who sides with whom and over what issues?

The system's operations may vary in terms of the rapidity and rigidity of its patterns of doing tasks. A family system may be observed in its patterns of operations in the initial session by the therapist posing the question, "What seems to be the problem?" The family members typically place blame on one another.

One can observe how roles are assigned and enacted, what issues are acknowledged, how problems are handled, how communications operate, how bids for power are negotiated, and where the alliances exist.

Rather than being caught up in the content of issues, which often varies and becomes extremely confusing, the family therapist looks first to the pattern of *how* issues are brought up and handled.

Communications, particularly metacommunications, act to maintain the structure of a system. Don Jackson (1964) noted that individuals are constantly commenting on their definition of a relationship implicitly or explicitly.

Poorly differentiated families have rigid rules about what can and cannot be discussed. When an unacceptable issue is brought up—one that is believed to be a threat to the stability of the system or its operations—the statement is handled by a stereotypic pattern or set of rules.

These metacommunications, which are never overtly spoken, are implicit in the operations of the system, and consist of intricate patterns of rules in which all content is subjugated. An example of this is, "No one say anything definite, so we do not have to acknowledge something we wish to avoid."

Family members may express conflicting messages and double binds, which are used to confuse and mystify. They may nonverbally communicate tensions to other members of an alliance, but if this is challenged overtly, it is disowned, disqualified, or mystified. Sluzki, Beavin, Tanopolsky, and Veron, (1967) classified types of disqualifications:

1. Evasion—change of subject,
2. Sleight-of-hand—whereby the response to an issue is so confusing that it is lost, and
3. Status disqualifiers—whereby an issue is discounted because the other is in a position of superior knowledge.

Additionally, nonverbal disqualifiers can be employed, such as facial expressions and silence.

These system defenses do not succeed in reducing conflicts. These avoidances end up producing symptoms that make sense when viewed in the context of the system.

From a systems theoretical orientation, the person's internal confusion fits the external realities. A person will have internal chaos since it is futile to make sense, when making sense leads to disqualification, invalidation, and rejection.

Interpretations may not be absorbed constructively, since they would become diffused, as would any other content. When the therapist enters the system, a healthier element is introduced. This begins to put pressure on the system to make accommodations. The therapist can build up selected members of the system, reinforce boundaries between generations, and strengthen the marital subsystem. As the system becomes better organized, it can deal with content with greater clarity.

Psychoanalytic theories such as object relations are historical and developmental, unlike systems theory. However, psychoanalytic theories and system theory share the belief that the whole is dynamic and more than the sum of the parts. They share the concept of a dynamic homeostasis that protects itself with resistances and defenses.

A therapist intervening at the system level does not work through the resistance, but manages it. This can be done by bargaining with the system and using paradoxical tasks.

At times, a therapist can bargain with the system, in exchanging one symptom for a less costly one.

The therapist might not evoke strong resistances with an acceptable bargain. For example, the therapist might suggest to a hostile spouse, "Instead of saying such nasty things, what if you vented a valid complaint in a very loud voice?" Volume may be less harmful than viciousness, but still allow for aggression.

In a paradoxical assignment, the symptom could be described and then prescribed as a task. The individual may even be asked to pretend to have the symptom, and to have the individuals involved in the symptom react in their stereotypic fashion. This serves to provide the system with a way to continue problem solving or relieving tensions without the threat of radical structural change.

When a person is asked to pretend to have the symptom, that person gains power without having to bid for power by being weak and having an uncontrollable symptom. The symptom is now something that he or she can choose to do. Additionally it puts the symptom in the control of the healthier conscious ego with its discretions and adaptations. The person might then ask, "Why am I trying to solve this problem in such a self-defeating manner?"

An effective paradox and reframing is at best an excellent psychoanalytic interpretation, since the unconscious often works paradoxically.

For example, the therapist might ask a passive-aggressive spouse to become even more passive-aggressive. For example, "Since you are not allowed to acknowledge your anger, you have unconsciously chosen to be 'peaceful' in a provocative manner that infuriates others. You are also helping your partner avoid depression. When you infuriate your partner, she, for a while, no longer needs to turn her aggression inward as depression. She can scream at you instead of at herself. Your assignment for the next two weeks is for you both to consciously, each day, play out your unconscious roles with one another. Steal the power from your unconscious and take charge of the inefficient ways you try to help each other."

This paradoxical assignment puts the person in a positive double bind. If the person does the homework by enacting the symptom, they are cooperating with treatment. If they refuse the assignment, they are moving toward the therapeutic goal of change. This can be used to get around resistances and reduce symptoms.

If individuals are insightful, then psychoanalytic interventions can lead to deeper changes and personal growth. Object relations theory allows for a much greater understanding of interpersonal relationships based on early attachments and the internalizations of relationships.

The locus of pathology in object relations theory is housed in the internal world of bad objects. Guntrip (1969) stated that neuroses are basically defenses set up to deal with internal bad objects.

These internal bad objects act gyroscopically to seek out others who fulfill our wishes and fears. Individuals seek to fulfill these expectations by seeking those who provide sufficient reality justifications for their transferences (unconsciously transferring emotional associations from parenting figures from childhood) and projective identifications (putting one's own emotions into another and provoking them to experience those emotions).

Guntrip stated that the depressive personality is still raging internally against the rejecting and frustrating internal bad objects. The depressive personality is afraid that hate will destroy the needed object and turns the hate toward the self.

The schizoid personality fears that not only hate, but also love will devour and destroy. (Kernberg [1976] would use borderline personality in this formulation.) The schizoidal core of personality is constantly oscillating between the fear of being engulfed and devoured by the object and losing the object. This puts the person in a conflict between the objectless world of nothingness, or the death of being absorbed into the object.

Guntrip believed that this results from a relationship with a mother who is alternately narcissistically impinging and rejecting. (Additionally, a child's temperament can also be a factor.) The emotional frustration proves too much for the primitive ego. The pristine ego splits into the central ego, which copes with external reality. The internal ego is left with the world of introjected objects.

The internal ego is further divided into the libidinal and anti-libidinal egos. They internally struggle between having needs and wishing fulfillment, and negating needs and refusing fulfillment.

These internal dynamics are played out in marital relationship as one spouse secretly hopes that the other will act to reject and deny needs according to internal anti-libidinal wishes.

Finally, the split-off and regressed ego goes into cold storage, and this regressed ego, which Winnicott (1955) refers to as the "true self," awaits a new love object or idealized parent figure to whom it can attach and grow.

All this draws off enormous energy from the central ego's ability to invest in the external world. In the infant's frustration at trying to master the external world, the child seeks to internally represent the frustrating needed object, as if to inoculate him or her with small dosages of the bad mother. However, the introject is too toxic and becomes a *fifth column* or *internal saboteur.* The introject becomes further split into the libidinally exciting, the libidinally rejecting, and finally the idealized object.

This idealized object is projected back onto the external object. The external object can then be pursued with less momentary anxiety. The infant can feel secure. This idealization is at an enormous cost, for it maintains the internal split of the immature aspects of the bad objects that are later projected onto one's spouse or child.

The idealizations are best maintained outside the realm of intimacy. The idealized love object aids biologically in the mating desires implicit in marriage, but quickly turns to bitter disappointment.

Guntrip describes the schizoid's dilemma of not being able to be *in* a relationship when the external object becomes noxious, but not being able to be *out* of it for fear of losing the needed and valued object. This *in-and-out program* may be reflected in the moving in-and-out of a relationship, changing of partners, or anything that promises an alternative to commitment.

Fantasies and infatuations with others are another way of preserving a sense of freedom from absorption into a devouring object. The schizoidal fear of being smothered, possessed, or absorbed leads to a greater fear of a positive loving relationship than of a negatively hostile one. Anger, disappointment, or disinterest presents a rationale for distancing out of a relationship and into safety.

Splitting of the needed object generally attempts to stabilize the internal world as well as the social world. To be "in" with the spouse may mean being "out" with one's friends, parents, or children. This represents an often-dangerous cost that psychotherapy hopes to resolve.

In the psychoanalytic relationship a person's idealizations, devaluations, black-and-white splitting of issues, disappointments, and fears become the focus. The person can develop a realistic ambivalence toward the therapist and then his or her parents. A realistic ambivalence (seeing all sides of a person) to one's self and intimates represents a higher order of structural maturity.

For healthy love to occur, a person must evolve from primitive concreting feelings of splits of all good and all bad objects. People need an existential emotional acceptance of humanity and its limitations and realistic possibilities.

Dealing with our family of origin both as internal objects and as real people, can help us love better. Yet people are surprisingly protective of the systems from which they originate despite their complaints.

Framo (1976) maintains that dealing with the real external parental figures tends to loosen the grip of the internal representations of these bad objects, which have been transferred and projected onto the spouse. Framo particularly stresses the need to acknowledge the love that may have turned to hate through disappointment.

The existential awareness of what can no longer be gotten from a person's parents and accepting them for who they are, helps an individual to go on and to invest in his or her spouse.

I suspect, however, that the key factor is working through the pathological idealization of the family of origin. All individuals retain an unconscious and defensively maintained idealization of their families, even the most embittered individuals. They often unrealistically wait for a healthy family reaction.

Within the context of therapy sessions, individuals can more objectively observe the original family's operations. They have a greater sense of the frustrations and hurts that came about and that give meaning to their oversensitivities and fears within the context of their marriage. The costly idealizations of their family of origin means displacing the bad object onto a spouse or child. By understanding the feelings that arose from the original frustrating love object, the intensity of the transferences and projective identifications (provocations) onto the spouse can become diminished.

Falling in love can be a hoped-for rejoining of the idealized but lost early love object. However, personality is still embedded in the original system. Thus, the spouse becomes the target of the unfinished hurts and aggression.

Marriage is a natural institution where individuals can regress. I try to turn the destructive regression into an opportunity for personal growth. The feelings in the relationship are often unconscious representations of emotional history and a person's internal object world.

I ask patients to differentiate to what extent their feelings are coming from their patterns and history and how much of their feeling are based on what the spouse actually did. Too much emotional reaction to a trigger can become a hint of transference, projection or projective identification.

The degree of affect often puts the situation into perspective. Spouses will find it easier to be empathic, once they reduce their distortions of the other.

Marriage can be viewed within the contexts of both object relations theory and systems theory. Object relations theory provides the understanding of the unconscious distortions and defenses that become intensified in a marital situation. The marital partner represents the internal, idealized and bad objects. Marital tensions arise out of the spouses' intensified cyclical transferences, projections, and projective identifications onto one another.

Systems theory views the locus of pathology between the spouses. Individuals are embedded within systems, and they will compromise their maturity by producing symptoms in order to stay emotionally within the original family. They will reenact these symptoms within the new family of procreation.

The combined view of systems and object relations theories allows for a wide range of intervention possibilities. The locus of the therapeutic interventions should be based on the accessibility of the patients. Psychoanalytic treatment for the more insightful patient will lead to the most personal growth. The analytic intimacy gets to the level of emotionally working through internal toxic objects.

The overall therapeutic goal is to change the marital system from a destructive reinforcement of the internal bad objects, to an opportunity to regress, exorcise toxic aspects of the self, and learn to love more maturely.

# Chapter 3 Measuring Individual Traits

One of the first things that a scientist does is to classify and measure. A good way to measure personality is with objective psychological tests. "How to Pick a Good Apple" was written by Debra Kay Woolever Bennett and me for the October 1986 issue of *Security Management* to explain in lay terms the MMPI (Minnesota Multiphasic Personality Inventory) and its value for security screening.

"The Insider Study," issued by the U.S. Nuclear Regulatory Commission (NRC), reported that of eleven incidents involving a potential threat to public safety during a three-year period, all were due to inside employees.

In its continued interest to learn about the best way to hire the right employees, the NRC commissioned a study. Psychologists F. D. Frank, B. S. Lindley, and R. A. Cohen (1981) found the Minnesota Multiphasic Personality Inventory (MMPI) superior to the polygraph, personal interviews, other psychological tests, and reference checks or recommendations when the criteria for tests included validity, reliability, compliance with legal issues, employee selection procedures, personal effects on the applicant, and susceptibility to faking.

The MMPI is a true/false questionnaire that measures many components of personality and is considered the best objective tool for assessing psychopathology. The MMPI has over 10,000 research studies spanning over forty years, including norms based on 50,000 medical patients from the Mayo Clinic.

MMPI scores are based on how individuals choose to respond to a pattern of items in comparison to how a known diagnostic group responds. The test was not constructed based on how psychologists thought people would react to different items. For example, psychopaths respond to certain questions on the Psychopathic Deviate scale of the MMPI in a characteristic way—they tend to deny things about themselves in a manner typical of psychopaths. The MMPI established norms for psychopaths and other groups.

Dahlstrom, Welsh, and Dahlstrom (1972) concluded that the MMPI has "proven to be more dependable across situations and across patient populations than human judges with different levels of training, different diagnostic philosophies, and different kinds of clinical experiences."

I (R. M. Gordon) saw the potential for using computerized MMPI reports in 1980 when the microcomputer became available. I developed reports that would generate objective decision rules for classifying test profiles as "pass", "fail", or "indeterminate" security risk.

After investigating the best decision rules to utilize in the report, I tested the predictive validity of these rules by comparing them to actual case studies. I administered my MMPI report to 52 outpatients.

The MMPI authors, Hathaway and McKinley, developed the MMPI for psychiatric inpatients. The original clinical scales are: Hypochondriasis, Depression, Hysteria, Psychopathic Deviate, Masculinity-Femininity, Paranoia, Psychasthenia, Schizophrenia, Hypomania, and Social Introversion.

In my computerized report, I added additional scales related to security risk. These scales measure: threat of suicide, violence, hostility, addiction proneness, blocking evidence of personal error, authority conflicts, resisting being told what to do, and poor work attitudes.

I also included positive personality factors such as intellectual efficiency, ability to tolerate confrontations, and self-sufficiency.[1]

---

[1] I correlated 150 MMPI scales with my sample of MMPIs so that I might better understand what the many scales measure. The results of this study is available at my online MMPI-2 interpretive guide at www.mmpi-info.com .

All testees were interviewed and rated on a scale of 0 to 3 where 0 indicated no risk and 3 indicated a definitive security risk.

The results indicated that all people considered a security risk were detected—8 out of 52 (100% hit rate). The decision rules also passed everyone who should have been passed. The decision rules produced an overall hit rate of 84%.

It is important not to fail someone just because of any psychopathology. However, indications of psychotic traits (poor perception of reality, confused thinking, delusions, poor emotional controls) and psychopathic traits (poor impulse control, hostility, addiction proneness, poor judgment, irresponsibility) are clear bases for a failure.

Assuming that a failure is any sign of psychopathology (any elevated MMPI clinical scale or indication of faking to look good or bad), approximately 50% of laborers and 30% of office workers would fail according to a sample of 3,300 nuclear plant workers. This would give too high a fail rate (too many false positives). After a clinical interview, a final fail rate should range between 1% and 5%.

Drs. Baird, Gerdes, Martenis, and I found that 132 out of 3,300 (4%) nuclear plant workers failed both the MMPI screening and subsequent interviews.

This showed that although many people experience emotional problems, few people could be considered potentially dangerous.

Personality states are brief. In contrast, personality traits result from a combination of inherited temperament and childhood relationships with parents. These personality traits usually endure for a lifetime. The MMPI measures personality traits that cause personal and interpersonal distress and impairment. The MMPI in combination with an interview is valuable in detecting possible personality traits that are associated with poor judgment, mood disorders, impaired reality testing, authority conflicts, hostility, paranoia, impulsiveness, and addiction proneness. Although it is hard to predict who will be dangerous, the combination of an MMPI and a clinical interview can scientifically narrow the field and help to select reliable staff.

However, assessment does not stop at a single testing. The management needs to have an ongoing recognition of emotional and stress problems in others. Supervisors will need to refer workers for assessment when they suspect an escalation of symptoms over time.

# Chapter 4 Treating Others Well

Love is not enough to maintain good intimacies. We need to treat each other fairly and respectfully or the love will fade. We reserve our most courteous behaviors for guests, while we tend to regress to our worst behaviors for those closest to us.

Over time, tensions build in relationships. Unfortunately, it is human nature to put more weight on disappointments than appreciation. We seem to habituate to love and care, and remain over-reactive to hurts. We often devalue and displace our frustrations onto intimates. Of course, we have our rationalizations for this poor behavior.

However, the standard of ethics is not based on rationalizations. The standard is best summarized by how you would want to be treated. People who consciously try to live by a reasonable code of ethics tend to have more contentment, better relationships, and meaning in life.

There are some basic universal ethical principles:

1. Do no harm.
2. Do good.
3. Self-care.
4. Respectfulness of other's autonomy.
5. Honesty, fairness, and justice.
6. Reliability and responsibility to others.

Psychologists make this implicit and sometimes explicit in psychotherapy. It is not so much what a parent says, but how that parent acts that affects children. The same is true for the psychotherapeutic relationship. The therapist needs to be a role model and create an ethical frame around the treatment. The therapeutic relationship is corrective and symbolic.

**"Ethics Based on Protection of the Transference"** was published in *Issues in Psychoanalytic Psychology* in 1993, after I presented this paper as an invited address at the Washington Square Institute. I was serving as a representative from Pennsylvania on the American Psychological Association's governing council when we were debating and voting on our revisions to our ethical code.

This revision of our ethical code for the tenth time since 1953 was necessitated in part because more psychologists had entered private practice. At first, our profession was dominated by researchers and not practitioners.

I heard during my Ph.D. program and subsequently from most of my colleagues, that there is no such thing as "transference and counter-transference." Yet as we debated a new ethics code, it was our own legal advisers who warned us to deal with transference and countertransference issues to help avoid ethical and malpractice problems.

The ethics code, despite the anti-psychoanalytic bias of most psychologists, had evolved to become more like the psychoanalytic ground rules. This revision reflects an unintended validation of standard psychoanalytic ground rules that are relevant to all treatment situations.

Freud (1915) described the ground rules of therapy and the boundaries of the therapist–patient relationship. The rule of neutrality is to help guard against the analyst's own problems, biases, and values from interfering with the treatment (countertransference). This is respectful of the patient's autonomy.

The rule of abstinence is to deny any inappropriate gratifications in the therapeutic relationship for either the therapist or the patient, so that the therapeutic work does not get derailed.

Freud understood that psychotherapy involves a therapeutic relationship that was both symbolic and real. For this relationship to remain therapeutic, the symbolic nature of it had to be protected. The patient would unconsciously repeat problems in the relationship with the therapist (transference). For it to be a therapeutic experience, the therapist must allow the patient to use the therapist as a symbol and as a container for all that is conflicted and unresolved. This transference of emotional issues needs to be protected and analyzed.

Fees are not looked at as something apart from the therapeutic relationship, but a critical aspect of the treatment itself. A patient can unconsciously communicate anger and power issues through payment and scheduling problems. If a therapist misses this, it sends a message that the treatment is only on the concrete superficial level of overt symptoms.

In the psychotherapeutic relationship, confidentiality and privacy are not simply a courtesy as in medical practice. The holding of secrets and forbidden issues are one of the most important factors in the treatment itself. The deeper the treatment, the more this is an issue.

For the unconscious to feel safe to unleash its secrets, there needs to be a very strict frame around the relationship. Extra-analytic contacts are avoided to protect the symbolic nature of the relationship. I often hear patients remember and reveal things they did not express in treatments that just focused on their symptoms and did not have a strict psychoanalytic frame.

No other psychotherapeutic treatment involves as many ground rules as does psychoanalytically informed treatment. Cognitive-behavioral treatments put the irrational thought at the locus of pathology. Therefore, the relationship and the holding environment are not central to the treatment.

Psychoanalytic theory puts the locus of functional psychopathology in early development and in the formation of a dynamic unconscious. Relationships are a critical factor in the development of symptoms.

Personality is the result of the external interaction with parents with the innate drives, affects, and temperament. The child forms good and bad objects that are the internalizations of the perceptions of primary relationships.

Intimate relationships are central to analytic thinking. Along with the psychoanalytic interventions (listening, questioning, clarifying, confronting, interpreting, and reconstruction of the emotional past), the therapeutic relationship itself may be the most important aspect of personal growth. The therapist needs to be the good container of the patient's affects.

Since intimate relationships often cause problems, the psychotherapeutic relationship needs strict ground rules. We all can regress in intimacy. We feel rage and passion in close relationships. Regardless of the type of psychotherapy, the same forces are in operation.

Psychoanalytic theory has evolved treatment conditions that are as inherently ethical as they are therapeutic. This is because psychoanalysis is not a science of what is conscious and manifest, but what is unconscious and latent. The unconscious personality holds primitive impulses that need to be integrated into a mature ego.

There is reason to expect problems when the relationship is limited to only what is superficial. People will always try to repeat the symbolic past in relationships. Psychoanalysis is based on this assumption and acts to protect the symbolic nature of the relationship. This promotes an ethical practice that is empathic with the needs and not the demands of the patient.

Psychoanalytic theory assumes that the patient will demand gratification from the relationship, but needs to work through the past in the symbolic relationship. To protect this symbolic relationship is to protect the patient's treatment.

Wallwork's recent book, *Psychoanalysis and Ethics* (1991), argues that Freud's discoveries have made us aware that unconscious motivations may subvert moral conduct. In addition, those moral judgments may be rationalizations of self-interest or expressions of hostility. He quotes Julian Huxley: "The greatest change since 1893 in our attitude towards the great problems of ethics has been due to the new facts and new approach provided by modern psychology; and that in turn owes its rise to the genius of Freud" (p. I).

Wallwork believed that Freud was critical of a hostile superego-determined ethic. He did feel that Freud's work supports an ethical theory based on a concept of regard for others, concern for the common good, and individual rights.

Freud once commented that people might disagree with his theories by day, but dream according to them by night. Likewise, many psychotherapists may be critical of Freud's theories, but will have to practice by his ground rules if they wish to avoid problems. The basic nature of people does not change from therapy to therapy.

**"Handling Transference and Countertransference Issues with the Difficult Patient"** was published in the *Pennsylvania Psychologist Quarterly* in 1997. It was part of several articles I published over the years for the Pennsylvania Psychological Association on the topic of ethics and self-care. Most psychologists (and psychiatrists) did not have their own insight psychotherapy as part of their training. Most were not even taught about transference and countertransference issues in school since it was considered a "Freudian myth" by the prevailing behavioral and cognitive-behavioral academicians.

Subsequently, too many got into trouble. In this and other articles, I explained psychoanalytic concepts to some psychologists who might be anti-psychoanalytic. I warned that they could be caught in difficult situations with patients if they do not at least learn about a psychoanalytic understanding of unconscious dynamics that occur in all treatments regardless of their interventions.

If I were to develop an MMPI type "Lie" scale just for psychologists, two questions would be: "Did you ever have sexual feelings toward a patient?" and "Did you ever feel like cursing at a patient?"

As with the MMPI Lie scale items, they mean different things in different contexts. That is, therapists would have problems with impulse and boundaries if they acted these items out.

On the other hand, I would not trust a therapist who said "False" to any of the above. I would consider that therapist too defensive and insightless about countertransference feelings to be a good therapist. I would also fear that such a therapist will eventually become symptomatic, by acting out or burning out.

The countertransference feelings, that is, the triggering of the therapist's own conflicts while doing therapy, are common. The therapist is a trigger for the patient, i.e., "transference," and the patient is a trigger for the therapist, "countertransference."

In addition, when therapists get into trouble with difficult patients, it is usually because they mismanaged the transference and countertransference.

I might ask myself why a patient is being seductive with me. Does she have an impulse problem? Is she trying to get control over the treatment? Is she trying to master Oedipal-developmental issues? What is she repeating with me in action that she is not yet able to use with insight and conscious language?

When I am feeling anger at a patient, I wonder why this patient is infuriating me. Does he fear me? Is he trying to get me to reject him? Was his need to fight with me his way of testing my ability to stand him?

I consider what feelings are being stirred up in me and how they might be affecting my timing, tone, objectivity, and interventions. This is using the transference and countertransference for better understanding of the patient and me.

I had a psychoanalysis. I drove about 60 miles to Philadelphia, 4 days a week for 5 years. More than any part of my professional education and training, my analysis has been the most useful part of my ability to do good work.

When I am stirred up by a difficult patient, I can get to my issues and self-soothe. I then can go back to my patient without acting out, getting too upset, or saying something dominated more by countertransference than empathy. I can remain a good emotional container for my patient.

I am not saying that every therapist should have an analysis regardless of their personal theoretical biases. However, I do believe that all therapists should know what triggers them, and know their areas of vulnerability and conflict. This is necessary to do good work. I am not sure how this can be done without some form of insight psychotherapy.

I have been working with psychotherapists for several years. When they act out or start to burn out, it is largely due to the issues that are stirred up inside of them, causing more symptoms than insight. I consider it important for every therapist from time to time to have a mental health checkup. Freud recommended that analysts return to analysis about every five years. This should be regardless of the kind of psychological treatment the therapist is offering, since any treatment will suffer according to the therapist's blind spots and personal issues.

Therapists are the toxic waste dump of their patients. It is very stressful, and therapists, like anyone else, use denial and rationalization when they are needy and regressed. Many therapists were raised in the role of a therapist within their family of origin, where they were expected to deny their own needs in favor of caring for others. Because of this, many therapists do not directly feel their unmeet needs.

Therapists can get in trouble acting out their countertransference— with sophisticated rationalizations. They can be caught in the powerful web of the transference and countertransference dynamics, and end up hurting people and destroying their professional lives.

The phenomenon of transference does not know a theoretical orientation. In transference, we unknowingly transfer the past onto the present. We all do it to some degree most of the time. Transferences are particularly activated with differences in power, such as caregiver–receiver, teacher–student, boss–subordinate type relationships. With greater degrees of commitment and dependency, transference is stronger.

The helping relationship activates the powerfully conflicted child–parent relationship, which is a powder keg of feelings. The patient does not care whether you are doing biofeedback, behavior therapy, or psychoanalysis; you will get the same transferences. It just may not be as overt as in analytic therapy. Nevertheless, the patient will still go through the same periods of honeymoon idealization, then devaluation, resistances, and acting out.

Just as children start out in love with their parents and by adolescence become profoundly disappointed in them, so will our patients go through similar stages of idealization and devaluation, and repeat the same traumas with revenge.

When patients see us, they are also distorting us in terms of everything that is unresolved in them and their past. This is regardless of your interest in this phenomenon. A psychoanalytic therapist uses these distortions as the focus of the treatment. However, the nonanalytic therapist gets the same reactions. These reactions, though not interpreted, should be understood and managed for the sake of the patient.

I often assess psychologists who were in trouble due to a failure to understand and manage transference and countertransference. They commonly said that they never learned much about it in graduate school, or learned that it was just applicable to Freudian theory. They thought that if they did not believe in it, then they need not concern themselves with it. That is like physicians saying that since they do not practice, as did Louis Pasteur, they need not concern themselves with germs.

Some psychologists may not believe in transference and countertransference, but the malpractice courts do. Mishandling transference and countertransference is often considered as an act of unprofessional conduct by state licensing boards and is considered an issue of malpractice by the courts.

While an analytic therapist would be expected to interpret and work with transferences, the nonanalytic therapist is expected to understand and manage transference. Managing transference starts with the acknowledgment that all relationships are objective and subjective, real and symbolic at the same time.

Your patients may stay with you through their distortions because they sense the reality of your maturity, fairness, warmth, and empathy. This may help them master their aggression when they need to hate you in the transference. As an analytic psychologist, I let this develop and then carefully interpret its meaning.

However, if I were doing behavior therapy, I would manage the transference aggression. I would do this by clarifying our roles, clarifying the treatment, and clarifying the ground rules and goals of treatment.

A hostile patient might say, "You are using me, taking my money and I am getting worse!"

The therapist needs to realize that while in the transference the patient has a diminished reality of the therapist. The therapist is perceived as a dangerous object to the patient.

This calls for a *reality clarification* by the therapist. The reality clarification serves to restore the reality of the person and role of the therapist and the reality of the therapeutic work. This is the primary way for any therapist to manage the transference.

In analytic therapy, this is an opportunity to go deeper into interpreting an internal bad object. Otherwise, just restore the reality of your relationship and go on with your work, whatever your theoretical orientation.

For example, the therapist might say, "You brought me your long-standing symptoms, and asked for my help. Your symptoms will continue to wax and wane until you can better control them. I can try to help only by your coming to these sessions, here in my office, and following our agreed plan of treatment. Now tell me more about what is upsetting you. I will try to help you the best that I can."

This clarification has the key elements of reminding the patient (they forget) that you are a psychologist and that he or she is the patient. They came to you for help for their symptoms. You do some sort of humble treatment. You are not their mother, father, bad self, or lover. You clarify the reality of the roles, tasks, boundaries, and ground rules of treatment.

You will need to frequently repeat this with patients who have poor reality testing. You bring them back to the present from feelings transferred from their past child–parent relationships.

All therapists can benefit from understanding that the patient will transfer feelings, memories, perceptions, and dramas from the past onto them. Managing transference means reminding the patient about the reality of the present therapeutic relationship. This will be a constant need with the difficult patient. They would rather repeat the past with you than change.

I am convinced that regardless of the type of treatment you do, the more you understand transference and countertransference, the more empathy you will have for your patients, and the more you will enjoy your work, with less chance of trouble.

**"Boundary: Protection, Limits and Safety"**, was published in the *Pennsylvania Psychologist,* in 2000. The therapeutic relationship requires a secure boundary that is neither too rigid nor too permeable. For example, when a patient gives a gift to the therapist, it can mean any number of things in addition to being a simple gift.

The acceptance of a gift could communicate to the patient that the therapy is on a superficial level, and the therapist is unempathic. Empathy does not mean being nice. It is about accurately reading motives that are unconscious.

Too rigid a boundary would be characterized by refusing something like Christmas cookies, or refusing to acknowledge a patient in an elevator. Either might cause more injury than insight. Too loose a boundary communicates to the patient that acting out is the better way to reduce tension, as compared to insight.

Parents need to provide both a physical and emotional holding of the child that provides a sense of limits and safety. For Winnicott (1965), the analyst's protective environment, conveyed by strict ground rules, allows the patient to test the limits and then feel secure to work on a level of developmental arrests, rather than focus on superficial symptoms.

Patients need to have and test limits to grow. Boundaries help to "childproof" the therapeutic milieu, so one is free to explore repressed and disown parts of one's unconscious self.

Children need warmth, limits, empathy, emotional containment, and protection in order to have personal growth, and so do patients.

## Ethical Behavior within the Couple

Couples tend to regress in intimacy and feel entitled to treat each other poorly. The basis of this behavior is usually rooted in immature personality traits and unresolved issues with parents that get transferred onto one's partner. I developed a workbook to help individuals better understand how their personalities affect their intimacies. In *I Love You Madly! Workbook: Insight Enhancement about Healthy and Disturbed Love Relations* (Gordon, 2007b), in the chapter "On Being Constructive," I discuss the use of apology and fair fighting:

### The Use of Apology in Relationships

People who favor primitive defenses have problems with a true apology. They regulate their self-esteem by externalizing blame. However, without an (1) insightful, (2) responsible, and (3) remorseful apology, the relationship remains damaged and does not heal. Emotionally immature people see an apology as a humiliation. However, the act of apology is an expression of maturity. It has the power to help heal wounds.

### Fair Fighting

All intimacies have aggression in them. The trick is to fight fair and constructively by learning to:

1. Lodge a complaint in a factual manner.
2. State how you feel and what you would like.
3. Express your emotions such as anger in a mature fashion.

4. Stay on the topic.
5. Fight to be understood, not to get your way.
6. Negotiate needs, weigh evidence.
7. Never be mean.
8. Take time out if things escalate.
9. Apologize and admit that you are wrong.
10. Resolve fights quickly and get back to getting along.

# Chapter 5 Medea and Parental Alienation

One way to abuse children is to use them for one's own dysfunctional needs. The children may be loved, but they are harmed by exploitive love. **"The Medea Complex and the Parental Alienation Syndrome: When Mothers Damage Their Daughter's Ability to Love a Man"** was a chapter I wrote that was published in 1998 in the book *The Mother–Daughter Relationship Echoes through Time*.

Dr. Gerd H. Fenchel ran a successful conference on the mother–daughter relationship and later asked if I wished to contribute a chapter to his book on the subject. That was the only type of family relationship I did not experience and I felt that it was a mystery for me. I did, however, have experience with the mother–daughter relationship through my work as a court-appointed child custody evaluator and as a psychotherapist.

I had seen the effects of a parent turning his or her (self-object) child against the other parent without justification. It is not only cruel to the alienated parent, but it produces lifelong harm to the child. It is psychological child abuse.

I first presented on Parental Alienation Syndrome soon after Richard Gardner published his first book on it in 1987. In 1987, I presented "Suggestions on the Use of the MMPI in Child Custody Evaluations: Case Examples of Detecting Paranoia in False Negative Profiles" at the 10th International Conference on Personality Assessment in Brussels, Belgium. I felt that Parental Alienation Syndrome involved paranoia.

Although Parental Alienation Syndrome is induced by mothers, fathers, grandparents, and same-sex parents, it is far more common with mothers. We are more likely to abuse the people who are most available and under our power. Men tend to abuse women, and mothers are more likely to abuse their children.

In my child custody evaluation work, I have seen many mothers aggress against their children's fathers by turning their children against him. In the process, they do great harm to their children. When I work with patients who were turned against a parent, they often have a great deal of resistance. It is as if their whole house of cards would crash down if they realized that they were wrong. The person's core sense of reality seems shaken; "If my mother lied to me about my father, then can I trust her love for me?" Therefore, there is a great deal of resistance to the awareness of having been brainwashed.

I believe that brainwashing by a mother is both more common and more powerful than that of a father, since the child's bond with the mother is usually more primitive. Such brainwashing and alienation usually leads to a lifelong problem with establishing and maintaining a healthy intimacy.

I will discuss the following topics: The mother–daughter bond, the Medea Complex (the mother's revenge against the father by depriving him of his children), brainwashing (repeating the learned hostility) and the Parental Alienation Syndrome (the children's pathological wish to please the "loved" parent by rejecting the "hated" parent). I will also discuss the subsequent disturbed intimacies that the alienating child suffers later in life, and a case history of three generations of Parental Alienation Syndrome.

I will bring together two separate issues: the Medea Complex and the Parental Alienation Syndrome. I believe that the Medea Complex in divorcing mothers is a frequent cause of Parental Alienation Syndrome.

## The Mother–Daughter Bond

Mothers are more likely than fathers to be alienators and brainwashers (Gardner, 1987). Mothers are more likely to take out their aggression on their children. Selma Kramer (1995) refers to Steele's research (1970) in stating that children are more physically abused by their mothers, and sexually abused by their fathers. Women may have fewer means of expressing power, and therefore may use their own children as scapegoats.

The mother's brainwashing of a daughter is particularly powerful due to the daughter's identification with the mother. Juni and Grimm (1993), in their study of adults and their parents, found that the strongest relationships were between mother–daughter and father–son dyads. Troll (1987) found that mother–daughter relationships "appear to be more complex, ambivalent and ambiguous than do other parent–child configurations"

Olver, Aries, and Batgos (1989) found that, "First born women had the least separate sense of self and reported the greatest degree of maternal involvement and intrusiveness. . . . Men showed a more separate sense of self than women." They also found that mothers were reported to be more highly involved with and intrusive in the lives of their daughters than their sons.

Gerd Fenchel (1998) points out that the mother–daughter relationship is a primitive latent homosexual one that is intense and ambivalent; one that requires first fusion, then separation for the proper development to occur.

When the mother encourages her daughter to see her father as bad, this can cause an Oedipal fixation in that the daughter may be attracted to men who will mistreat her, or she may mistreat them. The daughter will also have problems with separation from the mother and have problems with attachment and abandonment with subsequent love objects.

The son has his mother as his Oedipal love object, but is aided in his separation from her when he must go to his father for his male identity. The daughter is more closely tied to her mother as both a primary love object and source of her identity. Her Oedipal drive toward the father fosters development in helping her to separate from her mother and to master the outside world, which father represents.

If the mother devalues the father and sees separation as betrayal, the daughter does not make that necessary break from her mother. The daughter remains too attached to the parasitic mother. The daughter is likely to become insecure, dependent, and have love disturbances.

Fathers are very important to their daughter's feminine development. Biller's research review (1971) supports the belief that girls who had positive relationships with their fathers were more likely to have satisfying intimacies. When a mother poisons her daughter's love of her father, she is also damaging her daughter's ability to maturely love any man. The mother is programming her daughter to be her ego extension without a will of her own, and to be with her and no one else, narcissistically bound.

Although both boys and girls are greatly harmed when they are turned against a parent, the harm is often different. Studies indicate that boys suffer the most harm when they are stuck with mothers who express hostility toward their fathers—the source of their male identity (Kelly, 1993).

In keeping with the theme of the mother–daughter relationship, I will focus only on the mother–daughter bond in the Parental Alienation Syndrome. Although the daughter's self-esteem may not suffer as much as the son's may, her ability to deal with separation and mature relationships with men is very deeply affected.

Wallerstein's (1989) 10-year longitudinal study of girls from divorced families found that the nature of the mother–daughter relationship, and the daughter's identification with her mother, were predictive of the daughter's ability to have healthy relationships with men later on. Daughters who identified with hostile mothers had the poorest adjustment.

A woman has two internal sexual love objects, the mother representation—the original love object, and the father representation—the later Oedipal love object. Both affect object choice.

A man has a narrower band of attraction. His love for a woman will always be affected by his internal mother representation. He has his mother as his ever-powerful love object. His father is a latent homosexual love object and source of identification that does not play the same gyroscopic object role as does the mother. A man will not marry a woman like his father.

A woman, however, will choose a man in reaction to her mother and/or her father. If the daughter is turned against her father by a hostile paranoid mother (which is often the case), the daughter has internally two core love objects, the hostile mother and the devalued father. These internal objects will guide her love choices and her behaviors in relationships with men. By picking, provoking, or by distorting, she will try to repeat her emotional past with men.

At this point, I wish to make the important distinction between the *emotional past* and the *"actual" past*. Our neuroses may be based on real events as well as on false perceptions and fantasies. For example, the child is traumatized by the belief and not the reality of the "hated" parent. The child might consciously hate that parent, yet at the unconscious level, the child often secretly loves that parent, who was, in fact, loving. The "loved" parent may be loved on the conscious level, but feared and hated on the unconscious level.

A patient may start therapy claiming that she was traumatized by her father. She may later realize in therapy that her trauma was based on her mother's exploitation and hostility.

Why would a mother do such harm to her own children? The story of Medea may help us to understand such motives. The Greek drama served the purpose to entertain and be therapeutic. Plays were to provide a catharsis for the collective unspoken traumas and pains of the audience. These classic stories express most beautifully powerful human conflicts characteristic of our universal psychology.

## The Medea Complex: The Myth

Euripides wrote Medea around 400 B.C. It is a story of intense love turned to such intense hate that Medea killed her own children to get back at her husband for betraying her.

Medea was so madly in love with Jason that she tricked her own father, King Aeetes, who guarded the Golden Fleece, and killed her own brother so that Jason could steal the Golden Fleece. (Jason might have done well to consider how she treated her father and brother before he married her.)

Eventually, Jason left Medea to marry yet another princess. Medea planned her revenge. The chorus blames Aphrodite for causing all the trouble, in having intense passion turns to hate. (The Greeks displaced psychodynamics onto the gods.)

Medea offered the bride gifts of a beautiful robe and chaplet. When Jason's new bride put on the gifts, her head and body burst into flame and she died a horrible, painful death. When her father embraced her, he too burst into flames and died the same tortured death.

Medea then took her sword and killed their two children. The chorus, amazed at the degree of Medea's vengefulness, doubt that anything can rival a mother's slaughter of her own innocent children.

Medea escaped Jason with a dragon drawn chariot. She taunted Jason by not allowing him to embrace or bury his sons. She rejoiced at having hurt him so.

Fred Pine (1995) refers to Medea as an example of a particular form of hatred found in women. "Medea's internal experience is a compound of a sense of injury—a sense that builds to imagined public humiliation and a sense of righteousness. . . . The righteousness implied here in 'the wrong they have dared to do to me' has struck me clinically. It is a frequent accompaniment of hate and hate-based rage. I think it stems from something self-preservative ('I have been so mistreated that I have this right . . . ') and some flaw in the super-ego, possibly based on identification with the child's experience of the rageful mother's giving herself full permission—and without subsequent remorse—to express her rage toward the child" (p. 109).

That is, Pine suspects that for a mother to be so destructive to her own children, she herself must have been exposed to her own mother's unremorseful hostility.

Jacobs's (1988) paper, titled "Euripides' Medea: A Psychodynamic Model of Severe Divorce Pathology," views the Medea mother as "nar-

cissistically scarred, embittered dependent woman . . . (who) . . .
attempts to sever father–child contact as a means of revenging the injury inflicted on her by the loss of a self-object, her hero-husband." Jacobs feels that the Medea mother is dependent and that she cannot deal
with the loss. Therefore, she holds on to the relationship with hate.

Medea certainly has a flaw in her moral reasoning. We know this
early on when she betrays her father and kills her brother to help Jason
steal from them. However, she not only kills his new bride and her father, but her own children.

Medea's love turned to hate is so passionate that she destroys that
which intimacy between them produced. The hate goes beyond her in-
stinctive need to protect her own children. Medea must make Jason suffer more than she suffered for it to be revenge.

Jason: "You loved them, and killed them"
Medea: "To make you feel pain."

The alienating mother's rage is rooted in part in a wish to destroy
the child, whom she at some level resents being stuck with, and may
turn her rage into overprotectiveness as a reaction formation. She is unable to let her children separate from her. She tells them the harm that
will befall them when they are out of her control. The mother projects
her aggression onto the environment and then makes her children need
her protection.

When the mother wishes to punish the father by turning their children against him, she is also aggressing against the children. In her unconscious, both the husband and the children represent the same thing
(betrayal and potential betrayal), and destructiveness is wished on
them both.

In short, a mother who turns her children against their father probably has at least paranoid features within a borderline or psychotic personality structure (Gordon, 1987a). She cannot deal with the loss, and
remains tied to her (ex)husband in an intimate hate, and keeps her children tied to her out of fear.

## Brainwashing and Parental Alienation Syndrome

I agree with Gardner's (1987) assessment that many mothers in custody disputes do some form of brainwashing. I have found that mothers' attempts to turn their children against their fathers in custody disputes are common. I have also found that this is by far the most destructive aspect of divorce on children. I now consider parental alienation of children as a form of child abuse, since it leads to enduring psychopathology.

Kelly's (1993) longitudinal research of children's post-divorce adjustment found that the majority of children adjust to divorce, and older children express relief. Most symptoms last 6 months to 2 years postseparation, and usually only involve adjustment disorders. (I discuss this further in chapter 11, "Children of Divorce.")

Only about 10% of divorcing couples with children fight over custody. Of this group, at least one parent often has hostile, egocentric, and paranoid features. In a study of MMPIs given to parents in custody evaluations, the MMPIs of the parents who lost the custody dispute had significantly higher scores in Psychopathic Deviant (hostility), Paranoia, and Mania (narcissistic and impulsive tendencies), than parents who won the custody dispute (Otto and Collins, 1995).

Most children do adjust to divorce, except if a disturbed parent uses them as a pawn to punish the other parent. This traumatizes the child, its effects may be lifelong and often passed on generation after generation.

Gardner (1987) stated, "Although the mothers in these situations may have a variety of motivations for programming their children against their fathers, the most common one relates to the old saying, 'Hell hath no fury like a woman scorned.' . . . Because these mothers are separated, and cannot retaliate directly at their husbands, they wreak vengeance by attempting to deprive their former spouses of their most treasured possessions, the children. And the brainwashing program is an attempt to achieve this goal" (p. 87).

Gardner also feels that these mothers are aggressing against their own children by brainwashing them against their fathers. "These mothers exhibit the mechanism of reaction formation, in that their obsessive love of their children is often a cover-up for their underlying hostility . . . And when these mothers "win," they not only win custody, but they win total alienation of their children from the hated spouse. The victory here results in psychological destruction of the children which, I believe, is what they basically want anyway" (p. 87–88).

Brainwashing is a conscious act of programming the child against the other parent. However, Gardner went on to describe what he refers to as *Parental Alienation Syndrome*. The concept of Parental Alienation Syndrome includes the brainwashing component, but is more inclusive. It includes not only conscious but also unconscious factors within the programming parent, which contribute to the child's alienation from the other parent.

Furthermore, it includes factors that arise within the child— independent of the parental contributions. The child may justify the alienation with memories of minor altercations experienced in the relationship with the hated parent. These are usually trivial and are experiences that most children quickly forget.

These children may even refuse to accept evidence that is obvious proof of the hated parent's position. Commonly these children will accept as 100% valid the allegations of the loved parent against the hated one. "All human relationships are ambivalent . . . the concept of 'mixed feelings' has no place in these children's scheme of things. The hated parent is 'all bad' and the loved parent is 'all good'" (Gardner, 1987, p. 73).

Dunne and Hedrick (1994) in their research found that Parental Alienation Syndrome (PAS) "appeared to be primarily a function of the pathology of the alienating parent and that parent's relationship with the children. PAS did not signify dysfunction in the alienated parent or in the relationship between that parent and child" This study supports Gardner's definition of Parental Alienation Syndrome as a pathological reaction to a parent, and not a conflict arising out the real relationship with real abuse.

Gardner also refers to factors arising within the child who contributes to Parental Alienation Syndrome, such as the fear of losing the love of the alienating mother, since "the loved parent is feared much more than loved" (p. 90).

Additionally, Oedipal factors are sometimes operative in Parental Alienation Syndrome. A daughter may resent the father's new female partner, and may identify with her mother's jealousy and rage, and the daughter may revenge by rejecting him.

## Damaged Ability for Separation and Intimacy

A daughter has her mother as the primary love object. Then she shifts to her father as the Oedipal love object. These two internal objects guide her attractions and patterns of intimacy.

If she had a rejecting father, but a healthy loving mother, the daughter will have problems in her relationships with men. However, she has a good prognosis for overcoming this problem. If her mother was healthy, the daughter has a firm base from which to grow.

However, if her mother has a Medea Complex, the daughter is more likely to have a damaged ability to love maturely. Both her primary love object, the mother, and her Oedipal love object, the father, are internally driving her to self-defeating relationships.

To love a man is to betray her mother. She can only love as she has been taught and shown. The daughter will find unconscious ways to undermine relationships by repeating love dramas.

A person can unconsciously undermine love relations in three ways: *picking* (object choice), *provoking* (projective identification), and distorting (transference and projection):

**Picking:** Denise came from an upper-middle-class family. Denise's mother refused to let her father visit her after their separation when Denise was five. By the time the court ordered shared custody, Denise's mother had alienated her against her father. Denise refused to go with him. When she did go, the Parental Alienation Syndrome was so entrenched that she provoked fights so bad that eventually her father discontinued the shared custody.

She had seen very little of her father since, and remained very close with her overprotective paranoid mother.

Denise and her mother were very symbiotic. Denise was also very protective of her mother, sensing her mother's need for her. When Denise entered treatment at age 34 she had not been married, nor has she been able to be in an intimate relationship with a man for more than 2 years. She only had chemistry for men who were of a lower social class, who were rejecting or abusive.

She often suffered from depression and anxiety. She had trouble separating from her boyfriends. Denise was attracted to men who represented her mother's and her own image of her father as a "bum." Her attraction was also based on her attachment to her mother, who was exploitive and destructive to Denise.

These two love objects, her mother's view of the father and the hostile mother, both formed her attraction to men. Denise fell in love with men who were in fact both her mother and her fantasized Oedipal father—tainted by the mother. She alternately saw me as the overly controlling mother or as the rejecting abandoning father.

I actively confronted her trivial complaints against her father as evidence of Parental Alienation Syndrome. As she worked through the hostile transference in treatment, she began to realize how her mother had distorted her father, and how her mother had used and injured her.

Toward the fifth year of analytic treatment, Denise developed a warm trusting relationship with me. She was then able to feel deep attraction to and fall in love with a kind and reasonable man. When she felt irrational aggression toward him, she was able to use insight about her past programming. Denise also reconciled with her father and enjoyed a new relationship with him.

**Provoking:** Lora came to treatment for phobias and general anxiety. She had little psychological mindedness, and at age 37, though very attractive, had only rationalizations to explain why she had only short-term unhappy relationships with men.

She spoke about men as a typically disturbed gender. Her parents fought bitterly until their separation when Lora was 10. She lived with her mother, who told her that her father was mentally ill and often made fun of him. She saw little of her father, who she devalued as ineffectual and crazy.

When Lora would be in an intimate relationship, she would tell him that she was easy going and got along with everyone. This was far from the fact. She had little self-reflection. She would find the most outrageous ways to provoke her boyfriends. Even the meekest would be provoked to outrage.

At that point Lora would distort the events and project the blame for the conflict onto the boyfriend. She would tell him that he had distorted everything because of his personal problems, but that she could love him anyway.

Lora would commonly enact this with me. I would interpret her behavior to her, and she would somehow rewrite history and complain, "You are projecting your personal problems onto me. How can I get better if you don't have your own head on straight?"

Lora was able to repeat her emotional past by provoking conflicts in her relationships. She resisted any interpretations of her own aggression, or that she was distorting men as crazy and ineffectual. Lora was too tied to her mother to be objective.

She constantly tried to provoke fights with me. The transference was stormy, and she remained provocative and insightless. She soon dropped out of treatment, thinking that I was more disturbed than her, thus repeating her usual pattern.

**Distorting:** Sue entered treatment at age 46, with two failed marriages and many failed affairs. Sue's mother was diagnosed with schizophrenia and was hospitalized several times when Sue was a child. Although her parents remained together, it was a very conflicted relationship.

She did not feel close to her cold father. Her mother was unpredictable and was often paranoid about her father. Her mother viewed Sue's developmental stages as betrayals and guilt induced Sue for her attempts at becoming autonomous.

Her mother was hostile to her father and men in general, who were considered the sole source of women's suffering. (Although I define the Medea mother in the context of divorce, the Medea Complex can exist in marriage, where the mother has the paranoid perception of her husband as psychologically abandoning her. She will turn the children against him and damage her children just the same.)

Sue was high functioning in her job despite her borderline personality disorder. She is intelligent and functioned well in her profession, and had some close friendships. However, she regressed in intimacies. She became paranoid and depressed in her relationships with men.

She would become extremely jealous, demanding, intolerant of separations, controlling, and would have fits of rage as a reaction to imaged insults. She would drive even the most tolerant men away, and come to the conclusion that her mother was right all along about them.

She distorted the men in her life to justify her rage. She became like her paranoid mother when she was with men. Although Sue in her six plus years of treatment made great progress in her self-esteem and became less likely to fall into deep depressions, she still had the tendency to regress in intimacy. Like most borderlines, she stayed better compensated outside of passionate relationships.

Sue's reality testing remained good, except in intense committed intimacies, where the pressure to distort men became overwhelming. This distortion was rooted not so much in her relationship with her distant father, but more based on her terrifying relationship with her psychotic mother.

Distorting men allowed Sue to displace her unconscious anger at her mother onto men. Sue feared expressing anger at her mother. Sue also distorted men so she could eventually escape from terrifying intimacy. She feared that love would harm her, as did her mother's love. Sue projected her own aggression onto men. Destroying her relationships with men also helped to keep her psychically tied to her mother.

People can repeat the emotional past by picking, provoking, and distorting the love object to fit the internal unconscious love drama.

Although I have presented the ways that people repeat their emotional past as three separate psychological mechanisms—picking, provoking and distorting—they usually occur together. Individuals who are more disturbed provoke and distort more than higher-functioning individuals, who mainly repeat their past object relations by who they pick.

I have found that those people who have been alienated against a parent in childhood will have love disturbances. If they are to have a chance at healthy relationships, they will need to work through their love dramas in the therapeutic committed intimacy with the therapist.

Many nonanalytically trained individuals, not working with unconscious distortions, take at face value the patient's complaints and memories, and thereby reinforce the alienation and the love disturbances. Working with only the conscious is too superficial to get to the damage from early pathological attachment. Patients have a hard time putting into language all that they felt and that their parents implied or acted out. A disturbed parent uses language to rationalize and to distort reality. Interpretations can make sense out of confused emotions. The therapy also needs to be a holding environment with a good container. The therapeutic relationship must be long and intense to achieve the necessary personal growth.

Patients who have Parental Alienation Syndrome will frequently try to "divorce" the therapist, using the same or similar complaints of the alienating parent. The Medea mother is unconsciously feared and she becomes a sacred cow. The adult patient will at first feel guilt at any feelings of aggression toward the mother, and often blames the therapist for "creating" the aggression. The patient may project onto the therapist the wish to blame and punish the alienating parent.

Once the patient emotionally accepts that intimacy with the therapist is not dangerous, the patient will be able to take on their deeper feelings about the mother, and work them through.

However, when working with children with Parental Alienation Syndrome, the work is more concrete and reality based. Rather than working through the transference, a form of "deprogramming" is necessary. This is a deviation from the usual neutral analytic stance.

Young children idealize their parents as a source of self-esteem. The therapist at first needs to protect this idealization. However the therapist, after establishing a therapeutic alliance with the child, can begin to point out "errors" that the mother made. The therapist then humanizes the alienated parent through reality clarifications. Eventually, the alienated parent needs to be brought into treatment with the child. Sometimes the alienated parent and child(ren) need to go to a residential treatment facility away from the alienating parent. The goal is for the child to move from splitting the world into good and evil, to developing the capacity for a healthy natural ambivalence in intimacy.

## Three Generations of Parental Alienation Syndrome: A Case Study

Richard was raised by two parents with Parental Alienation Syndrome. Richard's mother and father were from divorced parents. Both his mother and his father as children were turned against their fathers by their mothers.

Richard's wife was turned against her father by her mother. His wife had Parental Alienation Syndrome, and later his wife turned his children against him and they would develop Parental Alienation Syndrome. This is not coincidence. This is an example of how unresolved issues unconsciously are repeated across generations.

Richard met his wife Kathy in college. Although Richard was attracted to Kathy, who was from a different social and religious background, he nevertheless unconsciously picked someone who was psychologically similar to his mother.

Kathy came from divorced parents. Kathy's father was an alcoholic and her mother was paranoid and provocative.

Her mother would provoke the father to beat the children. When he would beat them, Kathy's mother would act helpless and later align with her children against the father. She constantly included her children in her suspicions that their father was engaged in affairs. The mother used these suspicions to justify her own affair, for which she felt entitled. Kathy told her father about the mother's affair, which ended the marriage. They divorced when Kathy was a teenager.

Kathy had Parental Alienation Syndrome with her father after her parent's divorce. She remained tied to her mother, both hating her and feeling dependent on her.

Although Kathy felt dependent on Richard, Kathy was unable to feel love for him. Soon after they were married, Kathy accused him of having affairs, and believed that he was the cause of all her fears and insecurities. She, the same as Richard's mother, never said that she loved Richard. Richard rationalized this away as he had learned to do in his childhood.

After 4 years of marriage, two unplanned pregnancies gave them a daughter and then 2 years latter, a son. Kathy was overwhelmed by this second pregnancy. She regressed and became even more hostile toward Richard. She feared having children, and told Richard that she was afraid that she might abuse them.

Richard took an active role with the children, but Kathy began to interfere with his time with them. She would schedule activities during the times he was to be with his children.

During his analysis with me, Richard was able to accept that his mother was unable to love, and grieved the loss of not having had a loving mother. When Richard worked through many of the issues of his childhood in analysis, he was able to see how he had repeated his attachment pattern in his choice of Kathy as a wife. He had grown to feel deserving of love.

On their 11th wedding anniversary, he asked Kathy what she felt toward him. She admitted after 11 years of marriage that she never loved him. She said that she was unable to love anyone. She admitted that she could only feel hate for him, but added, "Don't take it personally."

Richard then left the marriage. They had agreed to joint custody of their son who was three and their daughter who was five. Richard agreed to leave the martial home so as not to disrupt the children. Richard naively thought that even though Kathy could feel only hate or emptiness, somehow in the separation she would become a friend.

Kathy withdrew all their money from joint accounts, changed the locks, and refused to let him see the children. Kathy told him that he would have to go to court if he ever expected to see his children again.

By the time the court ordered home study 6 months later, the children were brainwashed against him. He had always been involved with his children, but now the children were clearly more distant and cool to him.

The social worker who had done the home study had been recently divorced. She wrote her report in favor of the mother. The social worker had no understanding of psychodiagnostics or Parental Alienation Syndrome.

Richard petitioned the court to have Dr. Richard Gardner appointed the court's impartial evaluator. When Richard finally saw Dr. Gardner, he told Richard that he was biased in favor of mothers having custody of young children, since mothers' bonds with children are stronger. (Soon after, Dr. Gardner modified this belief.)

Gardner told him that he would have an uphill fight for 50% physical custody. Richard claimed that Kathy was paranoid and resented his happiness. He said that he would present evidence of her turning the children against him, actively working to destroy his reputation and his professional practice, and her attempt to drive him out of town.

Richard provided evidence of Kathy lodging a false ethics complaint against him to his local professional group, and spreading false rumors to his referral sources to destroy his practice.

Richard played taped interviews of colleagues stating that his wife was spreading false and malicious rumors about him. Dr. Gardner heard the chairperson of the ethics committee confirm that Kathy made a false complaint.

Gardner asked the daughter, then 6 years old, why she had to move from her home. The daughter replied, "Because my mommy was afraid that daddy would come and destroy my home. . . . He came over and put marks on our car. . . . Mommy said that she could never be happy until he was dead. . . . Mommy hoped that he was shot at the bank that was robbed" (referring to a recent mass shooting at a local bank).

Both the daughter and the son described their father as immoral, dangerous, and not to be trusted or loved.

Gardner observed in the sessions with the father and children, that the father was warmer and interacted more comfortably with the children and understood their emotional needs better than the mother.

Dr. Gardner eventually wrote in his report to the court that Kathy showed signs of paranoid delusions, that she was a fabricator and was brainwashing her children against their father. He also stated that if it were not for the father's prior frequent and positive involvement with his children, the Parental Alienation Syndrome would have been complete. He suggested that Richard have full legal custody and 50% physical custody.

In the years that followed, Kathy remained alone and did not get involved with men. She continued to undermine Richard's relationship with his children. When his children reached adolescence, they refused to see him or talk with him.

Richard had been sending both the children for therapy. After three years of both children not making progress in their therapy, Richard finally asked their therapist if he could be included in joint sessions with his children.

Each child had a long list of secret complaints they had not verbalized to their father. Consistent with Parental Alienation Syndrome, the complaints were trivial, exaggerated, or false memories. The therapist had inadvertently reinforced many of the children's perceptions of the father, taking much of their complaints of him at face value. (Some time later, that therapist was fired. The employing psychologist told Richard that the therapist hated her own father and had no relationship with him.)

The children's therapist had not questioned the distortions or inconsistencies in their complaints. For example, his daughter claimed that one Christmas when she was six, her father gave her coal for Christmas. His daughter said, "You thought this was funny, I tried not to show my hurt, but I was very hurt."

The father firmly stated that this never happened. This denial was evidence according to the children of their father's defensiveness. The therapist also thought that the father was being defensive. Richard gave his daughter the phone number of his friend who was there at the time, so his daughter might ask her if he ever had given her coal for Christmas. His daughter avoided making the phone call because she needed to maintain her negative view of her father and maintain her alliance with her mother.

The father told the therapist that he was certain that he had filmed the Christmas in question. In the next session, Richard brought a small TV/video player. He first played a scene about an incident recalled by his son that had occurred around that same Christmas.

His son claimed that Richard was brainwashing him against his mother by playing a board game that he distinctly remembered 10 years ago when he was 4 years old. The game was Richard Gardner's "Talking, Feeling, Doing Game."

The mother did not want the children to play the board game with the father. The mother told the children that it was a game to teach them to hate her. The board game, in fact, only encouraged the open expression of feelings without blame. His son internalized his mother's perceptions of the game and had false memories of it. After the mother's complaints about the game, the children refused to play any more such board games with the father.

When his son saw the very scene that he described on the video tape, he was first struck by how young he was at the time. He seemed confused that not only did the incident not occur as he had remembered it, but that his father was being supportive and sensitive to his feelings to love for both parents. The recording clearly showed him and his sister enjoying their father at the time.

The Christmas scene recording showed both children excitedly opening many presents and playing with new toys with utter delight. There was no coal, no sadness.

Both children were amazed at what they were watching. They had been certain of their vivid memories of 10 years ago, when they were small children.

In that session, Richard's daughter said that she might have remembered it wrong. The therapist was furious at the father. She questioned if this was the same Christmas that the children were recalling. The father reminded their therapist that they were Jewish. This one Christmas was celebrated at a Christian friend's home during the time of the custody evaluation.

In the next session, Richard read the section of Dr. Gardner's report stating that their mother had brainwashed them against him.

He read about her paranoia about the board game, and some of the blatant paranoid statements she had made. The daughter stated to her younger brother, who was still struggling with his feelings, "What he is saying is probably true. I know that now."

The children began to have occasional brief visits with the father. When the daughter went off to college, she wrote to the father that she never loved him and did not wish to see him again.

Richard's son wanted to work on their relationship in his last year of high school. His son lived with him for a few months before leaving for college. In retaliation, Kathy threatened to take the son's money and cut him off. Richard and his son grew closer during his son's college years.

Richard remarried. Kathy never got involved with anyone. Richard has a close relationship with his son, but has no relationship with his daughter. His son was able to have a long-term rewarding intimacy with a sweet young woman. Richard heard that his daughter has serious troubles with trust and intimacy similar to the mother.

This case illustrates that Parental Alienation Syndrome and the Medea Complex can continue for generations. I do not think it can be broken without working through the splitting of the all-good alienating parent, and all-bad alienated parent and going through a grieving process. Without these conditions, later love relationships will suffer and the pathological relationships will continue for generations.

## Research on Parental Alienation Syndrome

Since my chapter, "The Medea Complex and the Parental Alienation Syndrome: When Mothers Damage Their Daughter's Ability to Love a Man," was published, I have had several attorneys ask why I did not also write a chapter about fathers inducing PAS in their children. I remind them that my chapter was at the request of the editor of the book, *The Mother–Daughter Relationship Echoes through Time* (Fenchel, 1998), and had to be on the mother–daughter theme.

I also explain that PAS is unrelated to gender, but is more often found with mothers since they are most commonly the primary caregiver and therefore they have more psychological control over the children. Richard Gardner (2002a) felt that as more men move into the role of primary caregiver, the percentages are likely to even out. I did notice that there was no empirical research on father alienators, only mother alienators. Researchers were unable to find a sufficient number of father alienators to study.

There are also two competing theories of PAS. Richard Gardner (2002b) defined Parental Alienation Syndrome as:

> a childhood disorder that arises almost exclusively in the context of child-custody disputes. Its primary manifestation is the child's campaign of denigration against a parent, a campaign that has no justification. It results from the combination of a programming (brainwashing) parent's indoctrinations and the child's own contributions to the vilification of the target parent. When true parental abuse and/or neglect is present, the child's animosity may be justified and so the Parental Alienation Syndrome explanation for the child's hostility is not applicable. (p. 3)

However, Kelly and Johnston (2001) suggested a reformulation of PAS as a dynamic coming from the entire family system. They view the target parent as often (but not always) contributing to the PAS.

I wanted to do research to test if both father and mother alienators use primitive defenses (such as splitting and projective identification), and which theory of the target parent was correct, Gardner's (the *target* parent as the unjustified target of irrational rejection) or Kelly and Johnston's (the *target* helping to provoke the PAS).

The MMPI-2 is the most frequently used test of psychopathology in child custody evaluations. It is the most objective source of data on the personalities of the parents who are litigating over child custody. Therefore, I sought to collect a large number of MMPI-2s from cases of both father and mother alienators, father and mother targets, and father and mother control parents (who were also court ordered to have child custody evaluations, but who had no signs of PAS).

Ideally, the best type of research would be to randomly assign infants to potentially divorcing parents with borderline personality disturbances and to a control group of normal parents. Such a randomly controlled study would help us to be precise about the nature of the cause-and-effect variables. However, even if it were possible to do, it would be horrifically unethical. Much of the research in the social sciences involves naturalistic studies (observing and measuring in a natural context) and archival research (studying measurements from records) because we often study problems that cannot be taken into the laboratory.

In order to help control for the many possible sources of bias in archival research (such as "cherry picking" cases that support the researchers' ideas), we requested data from several forensic psychologists whether they used the diagnosis of PAS or not. We asked members of the Pennsylvania Psychological Association's (PPA) listserv and PPA's Custody Evaluators listserv to contribute MMPI-2 profiles from parents who were court ordered to be evaluated for child custody. We collected PAS and control cases from seven forensic psychologists from different areas of Pennsylvania. The sample size was 158 MMPI-2s, with 76 cases of PAS and 82 custody cases in which there was no PAS (control cases). As expected from previous research, there are far more mothers who are alienators than fathers. We used MMPI-2 profiles from 31 mother alienators, 31 father targets, 7 father alienators, 7 mother targets, 41 mother controls, and 41 father controls.

Again, to help control for possible bias, I asked two researchers who had no background in PAS to help with the study. Ronald Stoffey and Jennifer Bottinelli did the data coding and statistical analyses and both greatly helped with the write-up of the study (Gordon, Stoffey, & Bottinelli, in press, 2008).[2]

We found that mothers and fathers who were alienators had higher (clinical range) scores indicating primitive defenses, such as splitting and projective identification, than control mothers and fathers (normal range scores) in both our MMPI-2 indexes. It appears that the main

---

[2] I would like to thank Ralph Rosnow, who suggested a method he developed with Robert Rosenthal, which we used to statistically test our hypotheses. Their analysis allows the researcher to test complex nonlinear predictions. Dr. Rosnow taught me research methodology when I was a Ph.D. student, and I am still finding his wisdom priceless.

factor is the use of primitive defenses and not gender. Target parents
were mostly similar to the control parents. The results showed strong
support for Richard Gardner's definition of PAS with the target parent's
personality not being a significant factor in the cause of PAS, (see Figure 5.1).

Our research shows that alienating parents favor primitive defenses
that we believe are a main component of high-conflict custody battles,
the worst of which results in the childhood disorder of Parental Alienation Syndrome. Primitive defenses include the splitting of reality into
an all-good parent and an all-bad parent and projective identification.
Projective identification occurs when one denies personal faults and

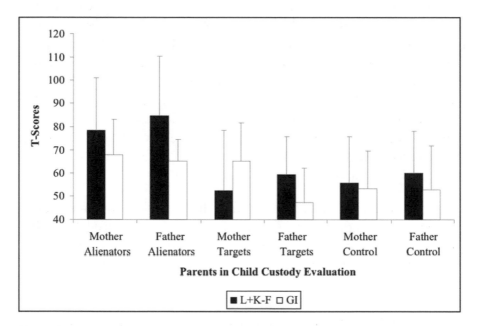

Figure 5.1   Bars show mean MMPI-2 T-scores (T50 is average and T65 is high), and
             lines show standard deviations of 158 parents court ordered to have child
             custody evaluations. L + K − F indicates denial of faults and splitting
             defenses, and the Goldberg Index (GI) (L + Pa + Sc) − (Hy + Pt)
             indicates a borderline level of functioning and the favoring of primitive
             defenses such as projective identification. There were 31 mother
             alienators, 31 father targets, 7 father alienators, 7 mother targets,
             41 mother controls, and 41 father controls. Alienating parents use
             primitive defenses, while the target parents are more like the controls.

projects them onto another, and then treats and provokes that person accordingly. For example, a child or alienating parent with irrational aggression infuriates a target parent so that the child and alienating parent can claim that the target parent has the anger problem.

We consider PAS as a childhood disorder caused by an alienating parent sharing primitive defenses with a vulnerable child against a target parent. The sharing of primitive defenses helps the child maintain a pathological symbiosis with the idealized alienating parent, who is seen as all good, while the target parent is seen as all bad. Projective identification is used to blame and provoke the target parent. We found little support for the idea that the target parent is similar in dynamics to the alienating parent. We hope that studies such as ours help in understanding the etiology and dynamics of PAS so that psychotherapists will know to focus on the use of primitive defenses in alienating parents and children with PAS.

# Chapter 6 Grieving Lost Love

We all have losses. Dealing with loss is part of living. People are often in denial about the love that was lost to them in childhood. They need to grieve their lost love. Without a grieving process, these people will have trouble with attachment and have love disturbances.

I wrote **"Recovering Bodies a Crucial Part in Grieving, Dealing With Death"** for the Allentown, Pennsylvania, *Morning Call* (July 23, 1999) after the editor asked to me write an op-ed piece for the next day. The following is an excerpt from that article.

The headline news today was that the bodies of John F. Kennedy Jr., his wife Carolyn, and her sister Lauren Bessette were recovered from the Atlantic waters off Martha's Vineyard. That story dominated the news worldwide. Their plane had crashed at sea last Friday night. After a few days the search and rescue mission changed to one designed to seek and recover their bodies. Why?

Why the enormous risk, effort, and cost to retrieve bodies? Can't we accept their deaths without the need to find their remains?

President Clinton instructed the Coast Guard to continue their search for the bodies, "because of the role the Kennedy family in our national life and because of the enormous losses they have sustained in our lifetimes."

I remember my incredible sadness at seeing little John-John salute his dead father, our slain president. I became connected to him in some remote way, along with millions of people around the world. John F. Kennedy Jr. was part of our nation's family. Now he, his wife, and sister-in-law were dead. It is tragic.

However, if ordinary people were in that small plane—no celebrity, no world figure—but just someone you loved very much, would not you do everything possible to recover your loved one's body? Why?

After decades, Viet Nam returned some remains of U.S. service men. It mattered. When remains are not recovered, loved ones wonder "could he be alive?" I still see "Missing in action, but not forgotten" flags and posters from people who hold onto hope that somehow he or she is still alive.

A patient of mine was convinced that John Kennedy, his wife, and sister-in-law had parachuted safely out of their plane, and were alive; that is, until today when he heard that their bodies were recovered. Then it was real. There was now no room for doubt, no room for denial. No chance for defenses to be creative. The recovered bodies made death real.

I recently started treatment of a young woman who was badly injured in a car accident. Her boyfriend died in that crash. He was her first real love. They were inseparable. They hoped to marry. She had no memory of the accident. She did not see him die. She was still badly injured and in the hospital when he was buried.

Her mother asked me to help her daughter; "she thinks we are all lying to her, she thinks he is still alive."

We need something tangible to help realize a loss. The dead body is no longer the person we loved, but it is a powerful connection to them. In our trying to accept the reality of our loss, we need as much reality as possible.

Death is so really hard to grasp. It was beyond the grasp of my patient. She said, "The last time I saw him, he was alive, how could he be dead?"

We need to get closure when we suffer. We need to face loss. Anthropologists have found that early humans ceremoniously buried their dead. One of the earliest functions of religions were to bring reality and meaning to death.

Recovering bodies can take many forms. Throughout life we must deal with a series of losses. If we do not recognize and grieve our losses, we can never really appreciate life. We lose people we love when they die. We feel great loss when love is not returned. We lose our feelings in childhood when we are not seen, heard, or understood. We lose our health, our youthfulness, and eventually our lives.

If we cannot accept the reality of loss, we get stuck, and we suffer. Depression is often the result of incomplete grieving. Rather than accept the loss of the love that you will never get from a parent, a child, and lover or a spouse, or get what we think is fair, we get depressed.

Depression is a way to go on strike against life. It puts your life on hold, and you are unable to connect and appreciate. Grieving fully and completely helps us continue to mature in life.

Recover the images of people you miss and let yourself cry. Let that help you live and love better. Recover bodies so you can bury them.

# Chapter 7 Personal Growth

What does it take to have personal growth? The answer involves such factors as insight, a therapeutic intimacy, and years of hard work. **"MMPI/MMPI-2 Changes in Long-Term Psychoanalytic Psychotherapy"** was published in 2001 in *Issues in Psychoanalytic Psychology.*

I rewrote this research article without the detailed methodology and most of the statistics. These can be found in the original article or on my web site at www.mmpi-info.com. I hope that I made this study more accessible, while retaining much of the science.

I have noticed in my work with patients in long-term psychoanalytic psychotherapy, that the Minnesota Personality Inventory (MMPI) and the newer form, the MMPI-2 (I refer to them as the MMPI/MMPI-2) showed profound changes to personality throughout the years of treatment.

These MMPI/MMPI-2 changes support the belief that the maturation of personality is only achieved from years of effective treatment.

The MMPI/MMPI-2 is rarely used to assess change in psychotherapy research, since the MMPI's scales tend to measure enduring personality traits, and most outcome studies involve short-term therapy. The highly stable MMPI/MMPI-2 is not likely to show significant changes in deep personality traits in treatment that lasts only 10 to 20 sessions.

For example, Smith and Glass (1979) in their meta-analysis of 475 psychotherapy outcome studies found that the average duration of therapy for these outcome studies was only 15.75 hours.

They looked at the connection between outcome measures and change from the treatments. They concluded that the MMPI had a minimal connection with the treatment or the therapist, and had a low reaction to the treatment.

They found that the MMPI's degree of reaction to treatment was low, similar to physiological measures, blind ratings, and grade point average. The highest reactive measures were the client's self-report and therapist's ratings of the clients.

Self-report scales that are obvious in what they are asking are highly reactive in therapy outcome research. When Beck was developing his cognitive-behavior therapy for depression, he found that the MMPI Depression scale was not reactive to his treatment. He developed his Beck Depression Inventory, which is very reactive to his short-term treatment of depression (Beck, Ward, Mendelsohn, Mock, & Erbaugh, 1961).

The MMPI Depression scale was developed with a criterion group, most of whom were in a major depression (Hathaway & McKinley, 1942). The items on that scale, as well as the other MMPI/MMPI-2 clinical scales, are associated with deep and complex psychopathology.

Beck did not get results from the MMPI because his treatment is not *dose effective* for deep and complex disturbances.

Cognitive-behavioral theory's premise is that thoughts are the locus of pathology. If one changes the thoughts, psychopathology will be cured.

Psychoanalysts feel that it is the other way around. Thoughts may affect our emotions, but emotions are not created by thoughts. Emotions come from many sources, such as biology, a lack of internalized good objects from childhood, developmental arrests, personality structure, and emotional traumas. The working through of emotional problems necessitates an intimate therapeutic relationship. A therapeutic intimacy is not an essential part of cognitive-behavior therapy.

Beck's cognitive-behavioral treatment is symptom focused and short-term. He encouraged a body of research that proves that his treatment works. As with my research on artifact in treatment outcome studies (Gordon, 1976), Beck created favorable circumstances by focusing on simple symptoms and making his own reactive self-report test.

The MMPI/MMPI-2 has not been very reactive as an outcome measure. This may be because most the MMPI/MMPI-2 clinical scales are based on enduring and complex personality traits that are stable for years.

## Stability of the MMPI/MMPI-2

The MMPI and the MMPI-2 are the most used and validated tests of psychopathology in our field (Graham, Ben-Porath, & McNutly, 1999, and Graham, 2000). Personality traits such as the Introvert-extrovert (Si) scale are the most stable. The Si scale, for example, hardly changed after a 30-year period (with a retest correlation of .74) (Leon, Gillum, Gillum, & Gouze, 1979).

After 5 years, 1,072 men showed high stability on their MMPI-2 scores (Spiro III, Butcher, Levenson, Aldwin, & Bosse, 2000).

Fiske (1957) found greater stability for the more extreme scores after 9 to 18 retestings on the MMPI. Subotnik (1972) also did not find a regression toward the mean with deviant MMPI profiles after 9, 21, and 33 months, with students who had psychiatric problems and were untreated.

A regression to a mean (or return to a normal score) occurs when there is an error in sampling or the finding is out of the ordinary. This is not the case with deep-seated disturbances. It follows that high scores in enduring psychopathologies, such as schizophrenia, should not become normal with just the passage of time.

There is very little outcome research on what is common in private practice psychotherapy, i.e., years of treatment with polysymptomatic patients. Psychotherapy that lasts for years is very difficult to study.

For example, placebo or no treatment control groups and randomizing patients to treatments would be grossly unethical and would constitute malpractice. One way to objectively study personality changes in long-term therapy in a private practice setting is to use the MMPI/MMPI-2 as a pretest control.

The MMPI/MMPI-2 does not show a tendency for a regression toward the mean or spontaneous remission. The scores are stable for years. Using the MMPI/MMPI-2 in the beginning of treatment can serve as its own control, which allows for an empirical assessment of long-term psychotherapy in an ecologically valid setting, such as an independent practice.

However, research with the MMPI/MMPI-2 as an outcome measure is waning (Hollon & Mandell, 1979) as is research on long-term psychotherapy (Stevens, Hynan, & Allen, 2000).

Brief therapy is easier and more frequently researched than long-term psychotherapy, but the conclusions are often not generalizable to actual practice.

A survey of the characteristics of empirically supported treatments (ESTs) identified by the American Psychological Association Division 12 Task Force on the Promotion and Dissemination of Psychological Procedures found that ESTs focus on a specific symptom involving brief treatment contact, requiring 20 or fewer sessions.

Traditional assessment methods, such as intelligence testing, projective testing, and objective personality tests such as the MMPI-2, are rarely used to evaluate these treatments (O'Donohue, Buchanan, & Fisher, 2000).

In a recent meta-analysis of 80 outcome studies, 79% were treatments of fewer than 10 sessions. The authors concluded that treatments should be at least 16 to 20 sessions to effectively study dose effectiveness. They also advise the use of uniform measures of proven reliability, such as the MMPI-2, rather than highly reactive self-reports (Stevens et al., 2000).

Clinical psychology is in danger of becoming the profession of brief superficial treatments for specific symptoms. It is also in danger of disenfranchising much of the effective long-term psychotherapy practiced by successful private practitioners with people who have complex and deep disturbances.

Seligman (1996) found different results by going outside the laboratory's typical short-term studies, by actually surveying 2,900 respondents who saw a mental health professional in the previous 3 years. He found that satisfaction with therapy was the greatest for those who were in treatment for 2 or more years.

Westen's meta-analysis (2000) put doubt in the value of short-term therapy for reoccurring disorders and polysymptomatic patients. Kordy, von Rad, and Senf (1989) assessed neurotic and psychosomatic patients in long-term psychoanalytically oriented treatment. They found that about 2.5 years was the most beneficial dose for patients overall, and about 3.5 years for the psychosomatic patients who stayed in treatment at least that amount of time.

Weiner and Exner (1991) used the Rorschach (ink-blot projective test) as an outcome measure with outpatients in long-term psychoanalytically oriented psychotherapy (in treatment 2 to 3 times a week for about 46 to 50 months), and with outpatients in short-term behavioral or gestalt therapy (in treatment about once a week, and no patient in treatment for more than 16 months).

They found that after the first year of treatment there was some progress in both groups. They retested all the patients again about 2.5 and 4 years after the start of treatment. The patients who stayed in the long-term psychoanalytically oriented therapy showed the greatest effects to their personality after about 2.5 years, and the changes continued into the fourth year of the study. The changes were extensive and profound. There were few changes in personality in the short-term behavior groups.

Most of the research on polysymptomatic patients and patients with personality disorders find that they require long-term psychotherapy. Psychoanalytic psychotherapy is aimed at personality structure and not just symptoms. The goal is to mature the underlying personality structure so that there is less need for a person to produce functional symptoms. This higher dose therapy takes time, but gets to the core of the problem.

Since the MMPI/MMPI-2 has not been supportive of brief treatment effectiveness, it has fallen out of favor as an outcome instrument. None of the current textbooks on the MMPI-2 now includes a section on the use of the MMPI-2 as a pre- and post-outcome measure in psychotherapy.

## Hypotheses

The MMPI/MMPI-2 should be significantly reactive to personality trait changes with only large dose, long-term psychoanalytic psychotherapy. The scales assessing deep and complex psychopathology, (F—Acute Psychopathology, Hs—Hypochondriasis, D—Depression, Hy—Hysteria,

Pd—Psychopathic Deviate, Pa—Paranoia, Pt—Psychasthenia, Sc—Schizophrenia, Ma—Hypomania, Si—Social Introversion, and A—Overall Psychopathology), should decrease after years of treatment. The K and Ego Strength scales, both measuring psychological resilience, should increase after years of treatment. (For definitions of these scales, go to www.mmpi-info.com). This is the opposite hypothesis of diminishing returns after the first few months of treatment.

## Method

Archival Retrieval

I am unaware of another psychoanalytic practitioner who gives patients, on a regular basis, the MMPI/MMPI-2 at the beginning of treatment, sometimes during, and at the end of treatment. I have been doing this for almost 20 years. This data has allowed me to help my patients to objectively assess their changes, outside of my perceptions and their transferences. I give it to almost every patient. I do not give it to patients who clearly do not want psychotherapy, but only wish a brief consultation or brief counseling.

As with any intervention, timing and empathy determines when I give the MMPI/MMPI-2. Most patients welcome the objective evaluation, and consider it part of their health care assessment. I have found the patients' reactions to the test to be analyzable. I have found the results valuable for both diagnostic and treatment progress purposes.

The MMPI/MMPI-2 has also provided me with data to test the reactivity of the MMPI/MMPI-2, with large-dose therapy. My archival field study is a practical way to do ecologically valid research on patients who were in therapy for many years.

A psychology intern took all the MMPIs or MMPI-2s from retired patient files according to the following criteria:

1. The patient must have had at least beginning- and end-of-treatment MMPIs. Consistent with most findings, many patients were in treatment for less than one year, and did not have a sec-

ond MMPI or MMPI-2. I typically do not give a second MMPI or MMPI-2 until at least after one year of therapy. Patients before 1995 took the MMPI, and thereafter took the MMPI-2. (I combined them by using raw scores and later converting them to MMPI-2 T scores).

2. At least one main clinical scale had to be significantly elevated at the beginning of treatment. The psychopathology had to be detectable by the MMPI or MMPI-2. Some patients had issues not assessed by the MMPI/MMPI-2 and therefore could not be included in the study, that is, child problems, adjustment disorders, etc. This criterion eliminated from the study some patients with ego-syntonic pathology (meaning that they do not detect their problems since the problems are too much a part of them to perceive) and some high-functioning patients with mild problems.

## Patient Characteristics

Fifty-five polysymptomatic outpatients (women = 27, men = 28) met the above criteria. The average age was 38 years. Eighty-two percent were college educated.

The average two highest scales were Depression and Psychopathic Deviate, indicating the sample's problems with affect regulation and healthy intimacy. The average duration in treatment was about 3 years.

The typical chief complaints were relationship problems (53%), depression (35%), and anxiety (24%). (The percentages do not add up to 100% because of the multiple complaints and diagnoses.). The most common Axis I diagnoses were: dysthymia 36%, anxiety disorder 25%, major depression 22%, and somatoform disorder 11%. The most common Axis II diagnoses were borderline 27%, narcissistic 25%, histrionic 11%, obsessive-compulsive 11%, paranoid 7%, and dependent 7%.

Ninety-three percent of the sample had some degree of personality disorder. Excluded from the study were individuals with psychotic disorders, substance abuse disorders (as a primary diagnosis), and antisocial personality disorders. This population is typical of outpatients in psychoanalytic treatment. They are bright, motivated, depressed, anxious, and have had long-term problems with relationships.

A subset of 18 patients (women = 8, men = 10) took the MMPI or MMPI-2 at the beginning of treatment, during the course of their treatment, and at the end of their treatment. The average length of treatment was about 5 years. The average time between the first and second testing was about 2 years.

This analysis helped to better understand when the changes to personality occurred. All the patients were in psychoanalytic psychotherapy at least once a week. Thirty-six percent were in treatment twice a week.

## Results

After about an average of 3 years of psychoanalytic psychotherapy, scales F (Acute Psychopathology), Hs (Hypochondriasis), D (Depression), Hy (Hysteria), Pd (Psychopathic Deviate), Pt (Psychasthenia), Sc (Schizophrenia), Ma (Hypomania, Si (Social Introversion), and A (Overall Psychopathology), all showed highly significant decreases in psychopathology.

Most of the scales went from the pathological level at the beginning of treatment to the normal level after 3 years of treatment. Scales K and Es (Ego Strength) significantly increased to higher levels of mature functioning. (See Figure 7.1. I pooled the raw scores for men and women and then converted to T scores. The graphs are in K-corrected T scores using MMPI-2 nongendered norms.)

Scale A is a very stable scale and a good measure of overall psychopathology. Scale A decreased by 50.3%. The F scale, another measure of overall psychopathology, decreased by 42.3%. The MMPI/MMPI-2 proved to be very reactive to changes in long-term psychoanalytic psychotherapy.

The scales of psychopathology (F, Hs, D, Hy, Pd, Pa, Pt, Sc, Ma, Si, and A) and maturity (K and Es) were not predicted to change in the early phase of treatment, but only after a few years of treatment. It is not clear from the above results when most of the changes occurred during the 3 years of treatment.

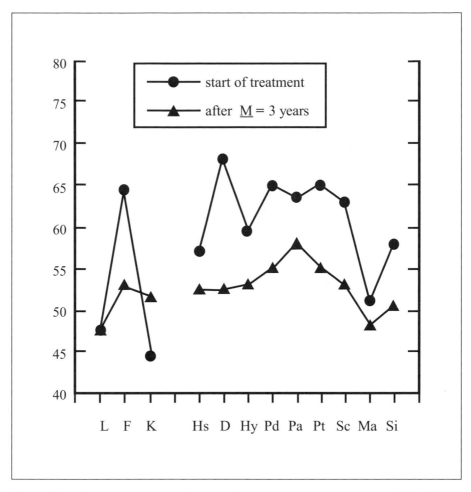

Figure 7.1    Changes in psychotherapy after about 3 years of treatment. T45–55
represents normal scores; T65 and above are high scores. The graph is
based on MMPI-2 norms using K-corrected T scores.

A subsample of 18 patients had more than two tests during the
course of their therapy. Most of the hypothesized scales did not significantly change during about the first 2 years of treatment, but did by the
end of treatment after about 5 years, (see Figure 7.2).

## Psychopathology, Ego Strength, and Length of Treatment

A more succinct way to present these results is to reduce the findings to two scales of the MMPI/MMPI-2, one measuring overall

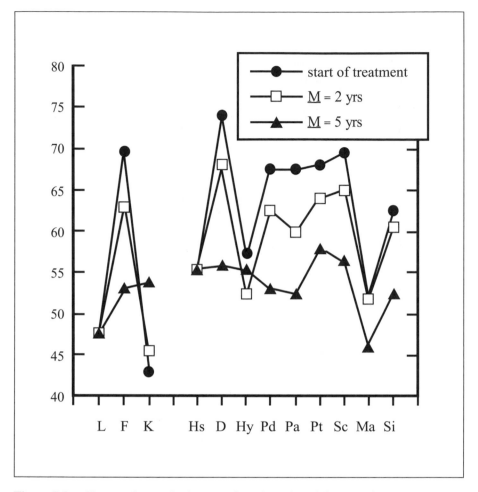

Figure 7.2    Changes in psychotherapy after about 2 and 5 years of treatment.
             T45–55 represents normal scores; T 65 and above are high scores. The
             graph is based on MMPI-2 norms using K-corrected T scores.

psychopathology (disturbance) and one measuring ego strength (psychological maturity).

The best overall measure of psychopathology is the A scale, which assesses the basic distress found within psychopathology.

The Ego Strength scale (Es) measures overall psychological maturity and resiliency. Es is a good measure of stress tolerance, resourcefulness, independence, discipline, and flexibility.

The A scale and the Es scale are very stable over years. In a retest study of 1,072 men over 5 years (Spiro III, et al., 2000), the A scale pretest mean was 45.95 and 5 years later was 45.5. The Es scale had similarly high stability, with a pretest mean of 52.3, and 5 years later a mean of 52.1. The two scales have a low correlation with each other, −.23 (Swenson, Pearson, & Osborne, 1973).

Scales A and Es did not significantly change in the early phase of long-term treatment. They showed no significant change after an average of 2 years of psychotherapy.

The results suggest that during the first year or two, acute symptoms may be reduced, but significant reliable changes to personality do not occur until after about 2 years of treatment. It is after about 2 years of treatment that a person's characterological baseline can change with intensive treatment. Patients continued to improve over the average of 5 years of treatment. They not only had significantly less disturbance, but also more psychological maturity, which is necessary to help prevent future disturbances (see Figure 7.3.)

## Discussion

The MMPI/MMPI-2 is the most used and validated objective test of psychopathology in our field. Yet researchers have found the MMPI/MMPI-2 to be a poor outcome measure, since it was not providing empirical support for brief treatments.

Researchers rarely study treatments that last more than 20 sessions. However, this study demonstrated that the MMPI/MMPI-2 was highly reactive to large-dose treatment, i.e., long-term psychoanalytic psychotherapy.

Most the psychopathology scales on the MMPI/MMPI-2 not only significantly changed, but they changed from being in the very disturbed range of functioning to the normal range of functioning after an average of 3 years of treatment.

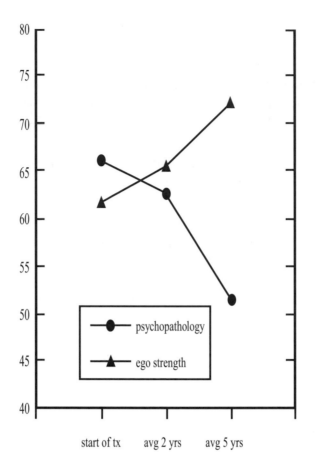

Figure 7.3    Patients on average needed at least two years of psychoanalytic psychotherapy to begin to make profound changes to their personalities. They
continued making reductions in psychopathology (as measured by scale A
[Overall Psychopathology]) and increases in personal growth (as measured
by the Ego Strength scale) into their fifth year of treatment and beyond.

There were major reductions in the areas of somatization, depression, intimacy problems, anger, narcissism, anxiety, identity confusion,
impulsiveness, and insecurity. There were also concomitant increases
in psychological maturity.

In other words, the MMPI/MMPI-2 not only showed a significant
and powerful decrease in psychopathology with long-term psychother-

apy, but also showed a significant increase in personal growth as well. Personal growth can be measured by the amount of self-reflective and self-soothing capacity, affect regulation, improved objectivity, and capacity for healthy intimacy.

This result is consistent with the literature, which indicates that the MMPI/MMPI-2 is not a good outcome measure for low-dose treatment. However, after an average of 5 years of treatment, almost every scale significantly changed for the better.

Looking at about 2 years, 3 years, and 5 years of treatment, it seems that on the average, between the second and third year of treatment, patients significantly changed in personality traits.

This is consistent with psychoanalytic treatment. During the middle phase of treatment, patients begin to work through deep-seated issues. This is when the patients begin to internalize the therapy, and make reliable, structural changes to their personalities.

It takes years to access some areas of personality because of defenses and resistances. On the average, it took about 2 years to begin to integrate these new changes into a person's enduring personality structure.

These findings—that deep changes to personality occur roughly after two years of treatment—are also found in other research, and are not unique to this study. This, however, is the first study to use the MMPI/MMPI-2.

These results support the value of not only long-term psychoanalytic psychotherapy, but the concept of phases of psychotherapy. A beginning phase is often characterized by the patient learning how to be a patient, and establishing a working alliance with the therapist. Temporary symptom reduction is possible in this early phase.

A middle phase is characterized by the patient going beyond talking about the manifest level of the symptom, to where the patient can begin to discuss and experience deeper levels of the problem within personality.

In this phase, the patient can assess areas that were unconscious and relevant to the problems, and use insight to not only reduce or eliminate symptoms, but to achieve greater maturation in the structure of their personality.

These results support the concept of a middle phase of working through deep issues after about the second year of treatment.

Finally, there is a termination phase that deals with loss and separation, which further aids in maturation of personality. All of life involves losses of some sort or another. The termination phase of a long-term therapeutic intimacy allows the patient to finish old losses and to prepare for the inevitable ones to come.

Some patients never get out of the beginning phase of treatment. They might be too concrete, not self-reflective, or too defensive for deeper reconstructive work on personality. These people may benefit from symptom-focused treatments.

In actual practice, one cannot be so specific about phases of treatment. Phases of treatment occur only vaguely in very rough periods of time. I did the therapy with all the people in this study. Some made progress in 2 years, where it took others 10 years to make similar progress.

Many patients seemed to have gotten worse before they got better. Many of the MMPI/MMPI-2s indicated an increase in problems at the second testing. This was usually due to the patient's increased ability to acknowledge his or her own pathology. The first testing often indicated a high degree of defensiveness.

Patients were often only aware of their manifest complaints. After a few years of working through resistances, patients' MMPI/MMPI-2s indicated less defensiveness and their underlying self-defeating traits became apparent to them (ego-alien). In other words, as the patients matured in therapy, they could take responsibility for their previously unconscious personality flaws, and begin to make maturational changes.

No two patients were alike in the rate they changed. Research such as this is useful to make broad statements about the necessity for high-dose therapy to help individuals with long-standing psychopathology. However, such findings are limited and may only serve as a guide when applied to individual cases, and may encourage those who doubt that such changes are possible.

Freud felt that treatment had to be intense, but that it was impossible to predict how long any one treatment might take. He referred to Aesop's fable of the Wanderer. One cannot tell a person how long it will take to walk to a destination without first noticing the pilgrim's pace.

However, Freud was not even happy with this metaphor, since "the neurotic can easily alter his pace and at times make but very slow progress" (1913).

Freud felt that the pace was based on what the mind could tolerate: "The shortening of the analytic treatment remains a reasonable wish. Unfortunately, it is opposed by a very important element in the situation—namely, the slowness with which profound changes in the mind bring themselves about" (1913, p. 350). Freud did not wish to focus on a person's symptoms, behaviors, cognitions, or coping skills, but rather to bring about "profound changes in the mind."

Profound changes in the mind, or what we would refer to today as profound changes in personality traits, are the goals of psychotherapy. A therapy that helps to mature a personality is not simply skill training, coping, or symptom relief. It necessitates a deep and long therapeutic intimacy.

Personality is necessarily resistant to change, as is our basic biology resistant to foreign invasion. The mind's resistance to change is basically a self-protective mechanism. It takes years to develop the type of therapeutic relationship capable of working through these powerful resistances to change.

Since these results are so similar to other studies, I believe that they are generalizable to other similar practices. The form of treatment in this study was psychoanalytic psychotherapy. It is well researched and manualized (Luborsky, 1984). It demands a great deal of training and supervision as compared to other treatments, but it allows for an understanding and treatment of enduring personality problems.

The majority of the public seeks brief psychological treatments for their problems, and there are many effective treatments available to them. However, many individuals suffer from problems that can best be helped by maturation in personality. Most of the patients in this study were polysymptomatic mainly due to their personality disorders. Brief treatments on each separate symptom would have done little to relieve their suffering. Many had been in symptom-focused treatment before coming to long-term psychoanalytic psychotherapy.

The distinction should be simple enough; brief cognitive-behavioral treatments have been shown to work well for many specific symptoms. However, many individuals may require long-term psychotherapy. The therapeutic relationship in long-term psychoanalytic psychotherapy fosters deep changes to personality that promotes a better ability to handle stress and intimacy, and promotes a greater sense of well-being. This study demonstrates, with a well-validated objective test, that this is possible after years of effective treatment.

What do psychologists look for in their own psychotherapy? Eight-hundred psychologists were surveyed. What psychologists valued most, from a list of 38 of the most beneficial things they got from their psychotherapy, was *self-understanding*.

The results of the survey had "specific symptom relief" as halfway down the list. Included in the survey were psychologists from all theoretical orientations (behaviorists, cognitive-behaviorists, psychoanalytic, etc.) (Pope and Tabachnick, 1994).

In a survey of 425 counseling psychologists (Gilroy, Carroll, & Murra, 2002) the majority of the respondents were cognitive-behavioralists. There were five times as many cognitive-behavioral therapists in the sample than there were psychodynamic therapists (*psychodynamic* is a form of psychoanalytic treatment). Yet the majority of the psychologists surveyed sought personal psychotherapy from psychodynamic therapists. Regardless how psychologists practice, they know the value of insight and a therapeutic relationship for personal growth.

# Chapter 8 Lies and Defenses

*Child custody evaluators: Psychologists or detectives?* is a book that I wrote, which was published by the Pennsylvania Bar Institute in 2002. This book is based on my presentation to the Pennsylvania Bar about the role of the psychologist as an investigator of specific allegations, such as child sexual abuse and spousal abuse. Many psychologists avoid investigating the accusations and focus on the current test results and observations. I advocated doing detective work.

I include this piece to show two things. First to show how I seek and weigh evidence; second, to show how love relations can become hateful and destructive when there are lies, primitive defenses (denial, splitting, projection, etc.), and little insight.

I often need to use psychological detective work to track down evidence in a child custody evaluation. It is not the type of evidence such as when a patient presents a symptom. As a treating psychologist, I try to find the symptom's cause. In my therapist role, I do not challenge nor try to independently verify the claims of a patient.

However, the examining psychologist in a forensic (court-related) role is often confronted with individuals who have reasons to lie. They will exaggerate their virtues and deny or rationalize their misdeeds. They present accusations of others and avoid admitting to symptoms.

The court in a child custody case presents to the forensic psychologist parties with accusations of neglect, violence, substance abuse, sex abuse, and so on. Diagnostic interviews, home studies, or psychological tests are helpful, but they cannot determine if someone engaged in a specific past act.

Psychological tests can hypothesize if such behaviors are typical or not of a given personality. However, very disturbed individuals may never hurt anyone, and some rather normal individuals may do some very bad things.

I use several different methods to go after specific relevant accusations. I employ interviews, surveys, standardized psychological tests, talking to witnesses, and reading documents such as police reports and medical reports. Sometimes my methods are unconventional.

Example 1

Two brothers, 8 and 11, both claimed that their father beat them with a plastic baseball bat and shot a gun at them to terrorize them. Children and Youth Services believed the boys, since their stories were plausible and consistent. The mother, who had left the boys with their father, now wanted full custody of them.

The boys had not seen much of their mother, and longed to be with her. The father was a hostile, gruff man who quarreled with the mental health workers. He stated that the mother and his boys were lying in order to be together.

I believed the boys, but I was still uncertain. The boys had been successful in convincing social workers and psychologists. Therefore, I presented them with a laptop computer with a voice stress analysis program on it. I had no literal faith in using this program as a valid test. However, I did tell the boys that it could tell if they are lying.

I separated the boys. I first asked the youngest boy to tell me again how his father beat him with a bat and shot at him. As he again related his story, I looked confused. I looked between the computer and the boy, saying, "Something must be wrong. It shows that you are lying."

I felt that the boys would not have the same confidence with a computer as they had with the "experts." Eventually he confessed that his older brother had practiced the stories with him. His brother promised that they would be able to live with their mother if they could fool the experts and the court.

I then went through the same bogus test with the older brother. I repeatedly stated that the computer was showing that he was lying. I also added toward the end, "Your brother told me that you told him to lie so you both can live with your mother. Maybe I can help you. But you must be totally honest with me." He then confessed to having fabricated the entire story.

The boys had no idea that their mother was mentally ill and was not a responsible parent. However, they missed her and they would lie to be with her. They saw their father as preventing this.

I called the brothers together and explained that they would not get into trouble for lying since they were so young. I told them that I would recommend that they see more of their mother, and that I wanted them to have the help of a therapist. I explained that the therapist would teach them to find better ways to solve their problems.

These desperate boys were particularly conning. Had I not been creative, I am sure I would have made the same mistake as the other mental health experts.

I remember in court when the mother's attorney attacked me for tricking the boys into confessing. I responded, "What I did is no different than what you do in court." The attorney angrily responded, "Yes, but you are a psychologist!"

Here are a few other examples of psychological detective work in child custody evaluations.

Example 2

A four-year-old daughter told her mother, "Daddy put his finger around my pee-pee, and he licks it." There was no physical evidence and the little girl later refused to talk about it to the Children and Youth Services investigators.

The investigators considered it "unfounded." The mother remained convinced that her husband committed sex abuse. This was the last straw in their strained married. The mother left the marriage and re-fused to let the father visit with his daughter. (Note that the suspicion of sex abuse was before a separation or custody dispute.)

In the interviews with the mother, she gave a consistent and plausi-ble history. My observations showed a close healthy relationship with her daughter. Her MMPI testing indicated that she took the test hon-estly and had a normal profile, which is consistent with her history and my observations.

The father was ingratiating and defensive in the interviews. His MMPI testing indicated defensiveness, poor impulse control, and im-maturity. He refused to take a polygraph exam since he said that it was a violation of his rights. He said that he was a Christian and that he would swear on a Bible instead.

Collateral witnesses stated that the father was immature and had a drinking problem. I encouraged the father to rationalize inappropriate sexual behavior by my saying that such sexual playfulness is natural and common in some cultures, and is often misinterpreted. The father then gave rationalizations for his touching his daughter, by stating that it was not sexual but playful, and that she had enjoyed it. He went on to state that his wife exaggerated what had happened to punish him.

I felt that the father probably had been sexually inappropriate with his daughter and was too narcissistic and defensive to have insight or remorse. I recommended only brief supervised visits and treatment for the father.

Example 3

After her two-year-old daughter's visit with her father, the mother claimed that her daughter said, "Daddy put soup up my bottom."

The mother immediately assumed that this meant sex abuse and filed a complaint with Children and Youth Services. They found no ev-idence for sex abuse, but the mother obtained a court order limiting the father to only supervised visits.

The father was wary of me, and was reluctant to have an examination by a psychologist. However, his MMPI indicated a normal personality. This was consistent with his history and my observations of him. He described his former wife as very suspicious. He said that she frequently distorted things so that she was often offended and felt victimized.

The mother was pleasant and seemed well adjusted. Her MMPI testing, however, was associated with paranoid traits. One collateral witness also described the mother as often misinterpreting even the most benign comments as slights against her. The review of documents was at odds with several of the mother's claims against the father.

The child reacted warmly to both parents. On the conjoint interview the mother's distortions and anger came out in a manner very different from when she was alone with me. When I asked the father to take a polygraph exam, he tearfully rose up from his seat, went over to shake my hand, and said, "Thank God for that opportunity. She has been making my life hell. How soon can I take it?" He did, and he passed.

When I told the mother that there was no evidence of sexual abuse, she felt that I was biased toward the father and that I had treated her unfairly. Because of the mother's paranoia, I recommended that the father have legal custody of the child.

Example 4

A father and stepmother seeking full custody of a 6-year-old child claimed that the mother was mentally ill and that she had physically attacked the stepmother during an exchange. The stepmother filed criminal charges against the mother. The MMPI of the mother showed that she had many emotional problems, more so than the others. (At this point, I believed the claims of the stepmother.)

The stepmother's mother claimed that she saw the mother attack her own daughter. However, when I continued to question her, she was inconsistent. At first she claimed to have seen the mother attack her daughter (the stepmother), and later stated that she did not actually see anything but heard the attack.

The mother claimed that there was no attack at all, and that the step-mother was fabricating. Usually people exaggerate, minimize, or ratio-nalize an event to serve their needs. However, it is rare for one party to say that they were attacked and press charges, and the accused party say that the event never happened.

I offered the mother justifications and rationalizations such as, "Did the stepmother start the fight?" The mother refused any excuses and just repeated, "It never happened." The mother also had her witness—her husband. He also said that there was no attack.

I finally suggested that both women take the polygraph exam. Both agreed. The mother took the exam and passed. The stepmother called and cancelled the exam at the last minute claiming that she could not get off work, and that she could not afford it. However she also added, "Besides I felt justified in this instance because she (the mother) was being so uncooperative, I wanted to teach her a lesson."

The stepmother ended up confessing to making false charges against the mother. (She later denied making that confession to me.)

At the advice of her attorney, the stepmother dropped the criminal charges, but a year later filed a child sex abuse charge against the mother. The judge referred the case again to me. Again I found the step-mother to be fabricating. I recommended continued primary custody with the mother.

Example 5

A mother claimed that her husband had beaten her. She said that she could prove that it happened since she had a protection-from-abuse order and the incident was on a police report. The mother was upset when I asked for a copy of that report, and accused me of bias since I did not take her at her word.

She stated that up until me, the pervious mental health profession-als involved in the case had believed her. She gave me her release to contact them. She saw their belief in her as independent support for her claims.

Indeed, my interviews with her therapist and previous custody evaluator confirmed that they felt that she had been beaten. However, they never checked into the police report. The previous mental health professionals did not consider her motives to lie, and they did not investigate her claims of abuse. The mother was a convincing victim.

I finally got a copy of the police incident report. It stated that the officers came to the home after the mother called claiming that she was beaten. The husband stated that she was lying and that she wanted him removed from the home so that her boyfriend could move in.

The police found no bruises or redness anywhere on the mother. The police refused to force the husband to leave their house.

Nevertheless, the next day the mother was able to get a protection-from-abuse order and had her husband removed from their house. Soon after, she moved her boyfriend in with her.

Her MMPI looked normal except that her Lie scale was much higher than the norms for custody litigants. The father's MMPI was associated with anxious, passive individuals.

Collateral witnesses stated that the mother was manipulative, and they did not feel that the father would ever hit her.

The father took and passed a polygraph exam, the mother refused to take it. The mother had alienated the children from the father, and they refused to see him. They made the visits with him very difficult.

I recommended that the father have legal custody of the children. I also recommended that the court appoint a mental health professional to help the children with their Parental Alienation Syndrome, with the eventual goal of the father having full physical custody of the children.

In all these cases, there is a parent with little insight and primitive defenses (denial, projection, and projective identification) who does harm to children.

# Chapter 9 Integrating Theories

**"Toward a Theoretically Individuated and Integrated Family Therapist"** was published in 2003 in the Russian journal *Psychotherapy*. It was based on the first part of my psychology lecture in Russia in 2001. Under Communism, there was little psychotherapy. The good of society was more important than the good of the individual. Personal growth was considered anticommunist. Russians often had a hard life. Many took refuge in spiritual and superstitious beliefs. There is no word for *insight* in Russian.

After the fall of the Soviet Union, psychotherapy began to take off. They sought American experts on the subject.

I focused my lecture on family therapy, which I felt was a good transition from the Soviet emphasis on the social unit to the new Russian emphasis on the individual.

My hosts pointed out to me that the 200 to 300 audience members (professionals and students) were sitting together according to their schools of thought. They already had rigid boundaries around their theoretical orientations. It was similar to how child learn religion, "Our correct one and the other wrong ones."

I wanted to warn them how such egocentricity of thought has hurt the advance of the science of psychotherapy in the West. I warned that it should not be copied in Russia. I explained that we hopefully mature as individuals from our family's biases. Similarly, as therapists, we need to individuate from rigid schools of thought.

I argued for knowing how all the main theories provide interventions useful for different sorts of people and situations. However, the best theory for understanding and formulating cases was psychoanalytic theory. It had the best theory for a deep understanding of people.

Although some patients might be too concrete and not self-reflective enough for psychoanalytic work, it is always valuable for a therapist to use a psychoanalytic formulation.

For example, is the personality structure primitive with mainly primitive defenses, such as denial, projection (putting the denied faults on to someone else), splitting (seeing things in black or white), and projective identification (provoking others to make them feel similarly disturbed)?

Alternatively, is the personality structure neurotic with mainly higher-level defenses such as repression? Patients who favor repression as a defense can respond better to interpretations than those patients who favor denial. With evidence, a patient can lift the repression and grow.

After the therapist has an understanding of the patient's dynamics, the therapist should then decide what interventions would best suit the patient. I advocate familiarity with all the major theoretical orientations and their techniques. I base the interventions on the needs of the patient and not theoretical biases.

Psychotherapists professionally mature by individuating from their theoretical family of origin. They learn to integrate concepts and techniques from most of the major schools of thought based on the needs of the family or patient. I will focus on the family unit as a pragmatic starting point, which can later lead to individual psychotherapy.

No one theory has been able to deal with the full range of psychological problems. I will offer a philosophical, theoretical, and personal review of the theories of therapy. Therapists can work from their favorite core theory, and branch out from that.

I will explain why I prefer a combination of family systems theory and object relations theory. These theories explain both the interpersonal and intrapsychic levels and each level regulates one another. The combination allows for interventions at either the interpersonal level or intrapsychic level, depending on the degree of accessibility.

The family unit helps to develop and shape individual personality, and each personality in turn contributes to the climate and operations of the family system. Understanding this linkage can help a therapist decide on which level to direct interventions—at the family system and/or the intrapsychic system level.

Sometimes the level of intervention is based on the degree of embeddedness in the system and level of psychological maturity. Children, for example, are strongly embedded in the family system. They benefit more from an intervention in the family system, as opposed to trying to appeal to their insights.

On the other hand, an emotionally sophisticated mother may be able to greatly benefit from the interpretive insights from individual psychotherapy, which can lead to improved parenting and personal growth as well.

Sometimes I begin by working on the level of the family system, reduce the symptoms displayed by the child, and subsequently address the marital subsystem or a particular parent in individual psychotherapy. I generally work from the larger, external family system and progress to an individual's intrapsychic system whenever possible.

I no longer believe, as I did as a beginning therapist, that all psychopathology emanates from the family dynamics. That was the prevailing belief in family therapy during the 1970s. Now I believe that it is far more complex than that. Since the 1970s, the field of genetics has advanced tremendously. We now know that much of one's basic temperament is biologically predisposed, and severe psychopathology, unless it is a result of severe abuse, generally has some biological basis. It was wrong to blame families for such disorders as schizophrenia, autism, and bipolar disorders.

However, primary caregivers shape the mind of the child. The family has its greatest influence on personality in the first few years of life. Research now shows that early attachment styles shape brain and psychological development. The capacity for self-soothing, affect regulation, and the healthy notion of self and others are developed in the early parent–child bond.

After early childhood, the family can cause stress disorders, worsening of psychopathology, or be a source of continuing love, guidance, and support.

Psychology seems most effective in dealing with the sequelae of psychological trauma. Perhaps the most damaging of traumas is from our own family. When the very family that should be the source of protection and love traumatizes a child, the damage cuts to the core of personality. Development is altered, and the capacity for healthy relationships is compromised. Interpersonal treatment can help the trauma that came from interpersonal causes, better than medication. Therapeutic relationships can best help to heal the repetition of bad intimacies that was a result of an unhealthy childhood relationship.

However, our field has been slowed down by having competing schools of thought trying to advance their superiority over other theories. Many therapists are often stuck in their early loyalties to a theoretical orientation.

If you wish to be a master of your profession, then grow beyond the assumptions and allegiances of your professional childhood. We help patients to individuate from their families of origin. Therapists also can benefit from individuating as well.

Studying the art of any practice involves some degree of identification and imitation of our teachers and gurus, who served as our professional parental figures (Gordon, 1995b). However, I often hear colleagues idealize their gurus while devaluing other schools of thought. This primitive splitting into idealized and devalued schools of thought represents a defensive insecurity and a lack of professional maturity.

I sought out and studied with some of the great proponents of the major schools of family and individual psychotherapy. Although I have my preferences, I can say that I have grown as a therapist because of my ability to understand, respect, and integrate the various schools of thought.

All our schools of thought are derived from long traditions in epistemological assumptions, and not scientific facts (Lana, 1991). These assumptions permeate academia and our present-day beliefs. The assumptions of behaviorism and cognitive therapy are that the whole of personality is the sum of learned behaviors. There is no dynamic unconscious or innate tendency. The best area of study is the observable behaviors or thoughts.

Yet the mechanistic assumptions that are implicit in behaviorism go back to the 17th century's British school of empiricism. The empiricist John Locke wrote that the mind is a passive blank slate, written on by the external environment. This philosophical view helped create a psychology of a concrete and simplistic model of the mind. This assumption is seen in the work of Pavlov and Skinner.

Psychologists mainly tested the behavioral model in animal lab research, and then generalized to the complexities of human personalities and relationships with often-poor results.

Behaviors are seen as the atoms of psychology, and that the sum of behaviors is equal to the whole of the person. Since the theory is based on a physics model rather than a biological model (as is systems and psychoanalytic theories), it developed no theory of resistance. This is significant, since symptoms often serve a function, and families and individuals are often reluctant to relinquish them.

From the opposite end of epistemological assumptions is the Enlightenment philosopher Immanuel Kant. Kant proposed a dynamic mind with innate structures and tendencies. The proper study of psychology therefore begins with understanding the innate structures of the mind and how the mind actively processes experience.

Darwin's theory of evolution gave us a structured brain that evolved from lower life forms, and took along with it a primitive inheritance. Darwin argued that mammals evolved behaviors and emotions for their survival value.

Freud then posited a structured mind with both primitive (Id), and anti-primitive, i.e. cooperative value-oriented structure (Superego), and a reality-oriented structure (Ego) to deal with the inherent conflict between the Id and Superego and the demands of external reality. In this model of the mind, the whole is more than the sum of the parts, since there are conflicting and dynamic interactions among the various parts of personality.

Freud considered innate character and the interpersonal-emotional world of the child. These forces are within the context of a dynamic unconscious mind with its defenses and its ability to encapsulate conflicts with symptom formation.

Freud derived his theories from case studies of mainly introspective, intelligent patients suffering from psychoneuroses. It remains the most sophisticated theory for understanding personality, symptoms, and defenses. The treatment, however, is not effective with concrete individuals who have poor self-reflective abilities.

When we view these different assumptions, ranging from the mind as a blank slate to a structured organizing mind, we can establish a corresponding continuum of psychotherapeutic theories ranging from behaviorism to psychoanalysis.

Systems theory represents a middle ground. It is ahistorical and its focus is on overt behaviors and not insight, as is behaviorism. However, similar to psychoanalytic assumptions, systems theory has a concept of the whole as more than the sum of the parts, with a biosocial model of resistance, boundary, and homeostasis, (see Figure 9.1).

These distinct schools of therapy, based on philosophical assumptions and particular patient populations (or animals), are often not generalizable to the wide range of human conditions.

| Locke | | Kant |
|-------|-------|------|
| Pavlov | | Darwin |
| Skinner | | Freud |
| **Behaviorism** | **Systems** | **Psychoanalytic** |

Figure 9.1   The Basis of Psychological Schools of Thought

Each school contributes valuable techniques and understanding of psychology, but none has fulfilled its original promise to be either fully explanatory or successful.

They can be unified under an encompassing theory that includes levels of systems, from the social systems to the intrapsychic system, from the level of overt behaviors to unconscious dynamics.

If one breaks out of the narrow school of thought, then a wide range of knowledge is available to understand and treat a wide range of psychological problems.

I started my psychology training with behaviorists. I began to break from my strict behaviorism roots by working with cognitions.

In New York I received supervision from Albert Ellis in rational emotive therapy. Ellis was one of the early proponents of cognitive therapy. He felt that most of personality is inherent and unchangeable, but what were changeable were irrational thoughts that could produce symptoms.

This led to a simple theory of psychopathology based on the assumption that wrong thinking led to psychological symptoms. Change the thinking and the symptoms will disappear.

The cognitive therapy model is from both lab research with human subjects and short-term case studies. It also assumes that only observable thoughts (a form of behavior) are the only or main legitimate area of study. There is really no theory of personality, development, resistance, or unconscious dynamics.

The interventions are helpful for most everyone. Most people feel better just knowing that they can control their irrational thoughts. Just persuade a client to remember that they need not be perfect, or need to have others approval, or need to be in control, and tensions may be temporarily reduced.

The theory does not seem to consider that these irrational thoughts may be a symptom of a deeper emotional trauma that needs emotion detoxification and the internalization of a healthy smoothing intimacy. This can only come from the context of a long-term therapeutic relationship.

Recent brain research shows that the science behind cognitive-behavior therapy (CBT) is weak (Panksepp, 1998, 2004). All mammals have similar affects that evolved because these emotions had survival value. These sub-cortical affect centers of the brain are not due to cognitions. Ironically, CBT therapists argue that they have the most scientifically based treatment. Even if their theoretical assumptions are weak and not backed by science, the technique is helpful.

In the 1970s, family therapy promised to become the great psychological panacea, and Philadelphia became the Mecca of family theory. I was fortunate to be a psychology graduate student in Philadelphia at that time at Temple University. To the south of me, I had the workshops at the Philadelphia Child Guidance Center with Jay Haley, Salvador Manuchin, Carl Whitaker, Harry Aponte, and Lynn Hoffman.

On the northern side of Temple University there was the Eastern Pennsylvania Psychiatric Institute (EPPI) where Ivan Boszormenyi-Nagy, Jim Framo, David Rubenstein, Geraldine Spark, and Gerald Zuck were developing their theories and offering conferences and weekly lectures in family therapy.

Philadelphia Child Guidance emphasized cure by changing the family structure and system. EPPI emphasized object relations theory in the context of the family system. I was geographically and philosophically in the middle of these two competing schools of thought.

As with cognitive-behaviorists, many systems-oriented therapists seemed to have an ax to grind when it came to psychodynamics, making it seem as though their ideas were in part a defense against the idea that there was an unconscious out of their control. Interestingly, it is the most controlling therapies that deny that there is an unconscious that is out of conscious control.

It makes one wonder about the motivation of therapists who solve psychological problems with more ideas of behavioral control than emotional empathy.

After my Ph.D., I studied with Peggy Papp at the Ackerman Institute in New York City. Papp taught me how to apply many of the quasi-hypnotic techniques of Milton Erickson to short-term work with couples. These techniques cleverly were able to deal with the problems of resistance that eluded the cognitive-behaviorists.

I discovered in my work with Peggy Pap that my talent for formulating paradoxical interventions was based on my understanding of a paradoxical unconscious. That is, I would tell a husband who was hostile and controlling, that he should continue that behavior since it was his compromise between his wish to be loved and his fear of it.

Generally, the paradox of describing and prescribing the symptom was enough to disrupt the behaviors. However, if it was also a valid interpretation of an unconscious conflict, it could also produce an emotional insight that helped bring about more lasting change.

I noticed that the other supervisees who formulated paradoxes that were not also valid interpretations of a self-defeating unconscious, tended to have less results with their families.

The use of paradoxical communication grew out of communications theory, which considered that metacommunications regulated a system. However, before that, there was simple communication theory, which involved teaching patients how to communicate more clearly and constructively.

The educative level of communications theory helps most families and couples learn on a conscious level how to better relate. This remains, regardless of theoretical bias, one of the most important therapeutic interventions; that is, teaching people how to speak clearly and constructively. It helps most people, most of the time. However, it is too superficial for families who resist positive change.

Dysfunctional families may use confusing and harmful communications to maintain their family system in a rigid homeostasis. Such families will resist such straightforward prescriptive interventions. Communication theory then evolved to deal with resistances, by moving to the level of (unconscious) metacommunications, which define roles, alliances, power, and boundaries.

Symptoms may be reduced by changing the communications with relabeling, reframing, and paradoxical directives.

At this point of my theoretical continuum from behaviorism to psychoanalysis is systems theory. Systems theory is not mechanistically based, but works like a biological system, which includes complex interacting levels of behaviors, not all of which are either conscious or have to do with learning.

Systems theory assumes that people are trying to maintain a homeostasis, not just responding to reinforcements. It assumes that biological systems resist invasions of their boundaries and operations.

Gregory Bateson, John Weakland, Jay Haley, Don Jackson, and Virginia Satir eventually saw metacommunications within a family system as a main cause of psychopathology. Double binds, confused communications, and mystifications could drive someone to psychopathology, even schizophrenia. These theories were largely based on observing families of schizophrenics, which often had poor communications. They assumed a cause-and-effect relationship without seriously considering that the members of the family of a schizophrenic may share some degree of loosening of thought. In addition, many families have poor communications, but do not produce a schizophrenic child.

It would seem to me that hostility, scapegoating, and negligence are more powerful in traumatizing a child than unclear speech. Based on these assumptions, relabeling schizophrenia as, say, *idiosyncratic confusion* was supposed to help this disorder. This theory, however, provides for powerful interventions to circumvent resistances and to help change patterns of communications that can produce damage to self-esteem and independence.

Eventually, while theorists such as Jay Haley focused on communication within a system, Salvador Minuchin focused more on the structure of the system. Systems theory does not view humans as simply made up of atoms of behaviors, as in the case of cognitive-behavioral theory and simple communications theory.

The family system is a biosocial unit that tries to maintain a homeostasis unless it is programmed to become open to change. The system has levels of power, boundaries, tasks, or operations it needs to perform, such as who does what jobs, how tensions are resolved, or how to manage changes in roles, membership, and alliances.

Psychopathology of an individual is based on the maturity of the family system. It assumes that such severe psychopathologies are usually a result of a family system with weak intergenerational boundaries, weak executive functioning, and unhealthy alliances (such as an overprotective mother), and the system's need for a sick patient to perhaps maintain or balance the personalities of the parents or take the focus from their marriage.

Salvador Minuchin based his theory from a population of acting out boys from the New York slums. These boys' families were disorganized and impoverished. Minuchin assumed that if their families became better structured, the children who were embedded in the structure of the family would become less symptomatic.

His techniques are often helpful for children of concrete beleaguered parents, who often have little psychological resources available for their children. I have found much of what he advocates to be much less effective with insightful adults.

Many of Minuchin's devotees have attempted to apply his theory, based on poor disorganized families, to insightful middle- and upper-middle-class families with poor results. These patients often complain that they felt unheard and manipulated.

However, Minuchin made it possible to make significant progress in the lives of children who could not be reached by techniques that involved theories of learning or insight. His techniques often help children get out of the role of the symptom bearer of the family with short-term treatment. Today, Minuchin adds a psychodynamic component to his theory by going into the parent's childhood. This allows for deeper work.

I felt that cognitive-behavioral therapy and systems therapies did not go far enough. I then went for psychoanalytic training. This also necessitated my own psychoanalysis. My analysis contributed more to my abilities as a therapist than all the other educational and training experiences.

The subjective relational emphasis within psychoanalysis is *object relations theory*. However, before I outline object relations, since it is a derivation of psychoanalytic theory, I shall first briefly review psychoanalytic assumptions. Freud held a concept of a structured and dynamic mind that was both selfish (Id), and socialized (Superego). This gave us a model of a mind in conflict with itself from the start, with the child dependent on both the adaptations of the Ego and the quality of the parenting to help reduce conflicts and move through the stages of maturation. Recently, research on infant attachment supports object relations assumptions.

The force to procreate and to protect is innate. The child is born with affects and drives that had survival value. The child needs the family to help tame these primitive forces. The child practices and needs to master issues of aggression and sexuality throughout development.

Rejecting, conflicted, or seductive parents interfere with normal psychosexual development, and the child traumatized by the family develops sexual and aggressive conflicts and fixations. The trauma is symbolically repeated in the symptoms. Later psychoanalytic theories added the importance of traumas with attachment and empathic failures. When the patient unconsciously repeats the trauma in the therapeutic relationship, empathic interpretations help the person work through the emotional past rather than repeat it.

This not only produces symptom reduction, but personal growth as well. Psychoanalytic theory is excellent at explaining many of the mysteries of human conflicts, defenses, and symptoms. It takes into account instinct, temperament, development, and family dynamics in the etiology of psychopathology.

In Freudian theory, the emphasis starts with our primitive drives. Object relations theory shifts the emphasis from innate drives to internalized parts of the self and others who are associated with aggression, sexuality, dependency, and love. Fairbairn (1952) felt that we are essentially social animals, not so much propelled by drives, but attracted to needed love objects.

These internal parts are made up of various aspects of the self and the external object (meaning the mothering figure for the most part, and later other family members).

These objects are not simple internalizations of real people, but subjective representations of them as perceived by the child's temperament, needs, and developmental stage.

The locus of pathology is housed in the internal world of bad objects and a compromised self. These internal objects seek out others to enact and repeat past traumas, or to repeat successful love depending on one's first loves in the family of origin. Individuals with family traumas have internal bad objects that gyroscopically pick, provoke, or distort current intimates to repeat the past (Gordon, 1998; Kernberg, 1995; Stierlin, 1970; Willi, 1982).

This theory is able to explain better than all others resistance and repetition. Why do people complain about their symptoms, yet are intent on maintaining them and resisting change for the better? Object relations theory helps us appreciate that symptoms help maintain the homeostasis of the internal object system.

A symptom is a compromise between the demands of the real world and the internal world of good and bad objects. It may be better for a person to have a lot of aggression in intimacy. It may represent the internalized need to punish the symbolic parent. Without such aggression, the person may feel extremely anxious, empty, or lacking passion.

Guntrip (1969) describes an "in and out program" for intimacy. The person may both wish intimacy and fear it, so therefore develops a pattern of moving in and out of intimacy.

When a primary love object frustrates and injures a child, later a dramatic and conflicted intimacy provides moments of familiarity and the safety from feared commitment. The person may need to attach to a drama, fetish, fantasy, a third party (child, lover, or substance), work, or an illness in order to regulate intimacy.

The self becomes split off into many parts as an attempt to give to the external loved object and yet retain some degree of true self. The person feels confused about his or her own healthy needs and the toxic needs of the bad internal objects. These internal bad objects become an internal saboteur that purposely seeks and maintains poor relationships.

Other theories do not begin to explain such self-defeating relationships, resistance to change, nor do they offer any enduring solution. Object relations therapy is aimed at the deep level of identity to which all relationships are subjected.

Although object relations theory represents the best combination of attachment and family context, temperament, development, and innate factors, its main drawback is that the theory is too complex for most therapists.

The application of analytic theories demands the most amount of training, often involving a personal analysis. It is intellectually and emotionally challenging. It is not a therapy for the masses.

Object relations theory has perhaps the best explanatory value of all the major theories of interpersonal behavior. It is the most sophisticated theory for understanding both pathological personality structure (such as Kernberg's work with borderline personality disorder 1976, 1980, 1989), and both mature and pathological love relationships.

However, its application is often limited to insightful psychologically minded people. There is nothing more powerful in helping a person grow than a well-timed, accurate interpretation of a self-defeating unconscious pattern in the context of being a good emotional container for the patient.

At this point of my professional life, I respect and work with all these theories. I hope not to have offended any of you in my trying to break old stereotypes in my oversimplified survey.

However, let me return to my point. To grow as a field and as therapists, we must give up our over identifications with schools of thought. I have found value in all of them, but none of them has been enough. After all my training in the various schools of therapy, and over 25 years of day-to-day practice, I have come to value most the combined approach of systems and object relations theories. This combination has the best explanatory value in understanding the complexities of human problems and intimacy.

Although I may use behavioral desensitization, cognitive therapy clarifications, and education in constructive and clear communications to deal with specific symptoms, I always use psychoanalytic formulations to help me understand the full depth of a person.

Religions and political parties are often stuck in their dogmas and splitting the world into true and false believers. Psychotherapists cannot afford such thinking. We are applied scientists. Scientists cannot be out to prove something, but only to discover with an open mind.

Our theories are guides in our thinking. We can integrate theories that range from external behaviors, internal conscious thoughts, a complex interpersonal system, to the internal dynamic unconscious system. All are interconnected. Therapists should not choose a theory based on assumptions and old loyalties. The choice needs to be based on what is the most effective and practical. Patients with limited emotional resources may be helped on a behavioral level, while other patients can be helped on a deeper level, and achieve more personal growth. Most therapists feel comfortable with ways of thinking that fit their own personalities. My best advice is after you have mastered at least one theory, to grow to respect other theories and techniques to add to your core modality. Your only identity should be the best therapist that you can be, and your only loyalty should be to helping patients.

# Chapter 10 Self-Esteem

**"Judge Psychology by Results and Scientific Studies"** was my op-ed piece for the Allentown, Pennsylvania, *Morning Call* in 2005. I wanted to respond to a recent op-ed piece by an English professor who wrote that the concept of self-esteem was pop-psych nonsense.

Again, I needed to write for the lay audience about psychology. I wanted to convey that although all people have their own theories about it, psychology is a research-based science. The following is an excerpt from my article.

Steve Salerno had a piece in last Friday's *Morning Call* in which he questioned the value of concepts such as self-esteem and confidence. He stated, "society has embraced concepts like self esteem and confidence despite scant evidence that they lead to positive outcomes."

I am a Ph.D. psychologist. I publish research and have been practicing professional psychology in the Lehigh Valley for about 30 years. I help people who have problems with self-esteem and confidence. Steve Salerno is a professional writer. People who are not psychologists are forever telling me about their own theories of psychology. In addition, I am sure that Mr. Salerno has many people telling him that when they retire they will publish a book.

I did a search of our scientific journals in PsycINFO on the consequences of self-esteem to test Steve Salerno's opinion. It produced over four thousand research studies. Almost all of the studies showed the benefits of high self-esteem and confidence. There were many studies that showed that higher self-esteem and confidence lead to better relationships, better physical health, better mental health, better incomes, and overall a better quality of life. The findings were neither scant nor inconclusive.

One study of 312,940 individuals showed evidence for higher self-esteem leading to better educational achievement and income. In a study of 471 mothers, researchers found that the low self-esteem mothers were more likely to abuse and neglect their children than mothers of higher self-esteem.

The findings were not limited to just our society. In a study of 13,118 college students from 31 nations, students took tests measuring self-esteem and other factors. The researchers found that self-esteem was associated with a person's life satisfaction.

A study published in the *Chinese Journal of Clinical Psychology* reported a positive relationship between self-esteem and mental health in 699 Chinese students. In a 2004 study of data from Russia over a five-year period, the researchers concluded, "Psychologists attribute a large part of well-being to self esteem and optimism. The same factors appear to influence individual's wealth and health."

There were also studies that did show the negative outcomes of high self-esteem and confidence. However, these studies were about the defensive distortion of self-worth, such as is found in narcissism, mania, antisocial personalities, and those with grandiose delusions. These are examples of psychopathology, not healthy self-esteem.

I would agree with Mr. Salerno if he had stated that self-deception leads to problems. People with unrealistically high self-esteem use others to maintain their inflated image and hence do not take negative feedback well, do not learn from their mistakes, and blame others for their own problems. I also agree that self-esteem and confidence are not substitutes for hard work, good values, discipline, limits, and concern for others.

Mr. Salerno wrote, "Pop psychology once taught us to wallow in our faults and limitations. It now teaches us to deny them, if not revel in them."

I would not confuse learning from popular psychology with learning from scientific psychology. However, an idea achieves popularity not by its scientific complexity, but its simplicity and function for the masses.

For example, research psychology has found parenting style will affect a child's self-esteem and confidence. The pre-psychology traditional *authoritarian parenting style* and its opposite—the *permissive parenting style* both produce children with distorted self-appraisal and emotional problems.

Research found that it was the middle ground style, the *warm-authoritative parenting style* with both love and limits, that tended to produce children with healthy self-esteem and confidence.

However, if what is translated into popular culture is simply "help children to have better self-esteem and confidence," then more good than harm can come from this democratization of the science.

I share Mr. Salerno's concern about pop psychology's oversimplifications. I feel the same way when politicians turn complex issues into sound bites. However, I would rather suffer some oversimplifying of ideas for the sake of public accessibility. In the end, the consumer will learn what works and what does not. That is true for science and politics.

# Chapter 11 Children of Divorce

**"The Doom and Gloom of Divorce Research: Comment on Wallerstein and Lewis (2004)"** in *Psychoanalytic Psychology* (2005) was my reaction to Wallerstein and Lewis's 25-year study of the effects of divorce on children (Wallerstein & Lewis, 2004, 2005).

Judith Wallerstein has several best-selling books on the subject of how divorce hurts children for the rest of their lives. I applied my knowledge of research artifact to argue that their correlational findings do not mean that there is a cause-and-effect relationship between divorce and later problems in the children of divorced parents.

Wallerstein and Lewis (2004) conclude from their longitudinal research of 45 divorced families, "This 25 year study points to divorce not as an acute stress in which a child recovers but a life transforming experience for the child" (p. 367).

The authors attribute the subsequent psychological problems in the children of divorced parents to the divorce itself as opposed to the psychopathology of either or both of the parents, the trauma of their parenting, and their stressful marriage.

They drew a causal relationship from correlational data, and give parents and those who advise them a very pessimistic view of divorce. Their conclusion is that divorce is the primary cause of the children's later life problems.

Wallerstein and Lewis used a comparison group of children from intact families who came from otherwise similar backgrounds as the children of divorced families. The children of divorced families had much worse psychological problems than the comparison group. However, this comparison does not help us understand what may have caused the problems in these children.

It would have been more helpful if the authors compared children from divorced families in which neither parent suffered from mental illness, with children from intact families with at least one mentally ill parent.

Wallerstein and Lewis blame divorce for the later psychological problems of the children without considering the more likely conclusion that the same factors that contributed to divorce also contributed to the emotional problems in the children of divorce.

It is difficult to remain married to an individual whose mental illness involves abuse, meanness, addictions, defensiveness, neglect of children, lack of empathy, selfishness, and remoteness. A mentally ill parent can influence the child both genetically and by the early and continuing traumatic environment.

Wallerstein and Lewis conclude that children of divorced parents go on to have poor relationships. However, it is more likely that temperament and the quality of bonding and parenting affect how well adults attach to others.

Waters, Merrick, Treboux, Crowell, and Albersheim (2000) looked at relationship patterns in 50 young adults who were studied 20 years earlier as infants. Overall, 72% of the infants received the same secure versus insecure attachment classification in early adulthood.

Additionally, negative life experiences also affected the type of adult attachment, such as loss of a parent, parental divorce, life-threatening illness of a parent or the child, parental psychiatric disorder, and physical or sexual abuse by a family member.

Kelly's (1993) review of 10 years of research on children's later adjustment found that many of the psychological symptoms seen in children of divorce could be accounted for in the years prior to the divorce. Kelly concluded, "the view that divorce per se is the major cause of these symptoms must be reconsidered in light of newer research documenting the negative effects of troubled marriages on children."

Hetherington, & Stanley (1999) found that although soon after divorce, children display more symptoms than those in high-conflict non-divorced families, but as the children adapt to the new situation, the pattern of differences reverses. When divorce involves children moving into a less stressful situation, children from divorced families show similar adjustment to those in normal intact families.

It is not surprising to hear children complain about the divorce of their parents, as expressed in Wallerstein and Lewis's anecdotal interviews. Children are often not able to as easily discern the psychopathologies of their parents as they can a concrete trauma such as divorce. The children of divorce might more easily talk about the divorce than the dysfunctional aspects of the parent(s) who caused both the divorce and their problems.

Wallerstein and Lewis promote a rather pessimistic and unbalanced view of divorce that can give false evidence for extremist, religious, and political groups to pressure families to remain together, often in contraindication to the safety and the welfare of the children.

There are many children who would rather escape from a toxic family system than remain in one. A divorcing parent could model that resolving trauma in a supportive relationship, which can lead to ego resiliency and a better life.

# Chapter 12 Toward Healthier Intimacies

Sections from my book: *I Love You Madly! On Passion, Personality and Personal Growth.* (2006)

From chapter 2, "Disturbances in Love Relations":

Otto Kernberg (1974, 1976, 1980, 1995) wrote of two basic love pathologies found in the most disturbed individuals: the inability to fall in love and the inability to remain in love. Another psychoanalyst, Salman Akhtar (1999) had added three more: the tendency to fall in love with the "wrong" kinds of people, the inability to fall out of love and the inability to feel loved.

The most severe form of love disturbance is the inability to fall in love. In order to fall in love some degree of idealization or overvaluing is necessary. In normal love, the idealization is primarily based on real qualities. In pathological cases, the idealization is extreme and can become delusional with an equal but opposite devaluation lurking beneath. However people who cannot fall in love at all either cannot feel an idealization of another or the idealization is a fickle and fleeting fantasy.

Individuals may have problems falling in love because:

1. They are egocentric, lacking the capacity to love another.
2. They dread closeness, since they associate it with the destruction of their fragile psychological world.

The next level of disturbance is when a person can fall in love but cannot remain in love. Personalities that fall into this category have the capacity for idealization and erotic desire. They unconsciously seek a magical love that is worthy of their grandiose self and also a rescuer that is transformational. However, they experience a great deal of hostility when the idealized love object does not live up to the hoped for magical transformation. They may become obsessed with deficiencies in the love object. They often fear that intimacy will reveal that they are a fraud and may project this onto the love object and come to see the formally idealized lover as a fraud. A cycle of idealization and devaluation of the other moves the person in and out of closeness. There is no true intimacy with a real person. This type of love is mainly a child's fantasy. They fall in love with a fantasy and then punish the real person for not fulfilling the fantasy.

Individuals may evolve from not being able to fall in love, to being able to fall in love but not remain in love. They might fall in love with the "wrong people" in service to their unconscious need to not remain in love.

As I enter my waiting room, I see Karen looking unhappy to see me. I brace myself as I remember her from the past. I enjoy doing deep and meaningful psychoanalytic work. Even after many years, it still stimulates me intellectually and emotionally, making me feel fortunate to have such a rewarding profession. But some patients try to drive me crazy, while I try to drive them sane. Karen feels empowered by defeating me. She sees her defensiveness as a strength.

Karen changes therapists the same way she changes men. She starts out expecting magic and when she does not get it, she devalues the person. She had been in and out of psychotherapy of one sort or another (some bizarre) since she was a teenager. When I first saw her briefly a few years ago, she was quoting from several self-help books to help her find a man. She read some passages in order to educate me. She could not understand why I had not read those books and still considered myself a serious professional. She particularly liked advice that is deceptive and manipulative. That sort of advice made sense to her. She justified her dishonesty since she assumed that men are innately untrustworthy. She was unhappy when I told her that I would not help her with deception, but I might help her to see what she was doing wrong.

Karen, looking around my office with a disapproving face says, "Dr. Gordon, I came back to you because I tried everything else."

"It's been about four years," I say. "You didn't seem happy with me before."

"I don't believe in Freud and going into the past."

Karen is really saying, "Just give me the answers, but don't ask me to look at myself." People who do not believe in Freud have probably not read or understood much of what he actually said. His theories warn that people pay a price for lying to themselves. Defensive people do not like to hear that.

Karen, now 39, never married. Her love relationships rarely last more than a few months. The longest was with a married man for 2 years. The fact that he was unavailable may have helped it last that long. When he broke it off, Karen got depressed. That is when I first saw her. She stayed a few months. When she fell in love again, she left therapy.

Karen's blue eyes scan my face for hints of my feelings about her. She had punky short blond hair and several earrings on each ear. Karen is still skinny like a teenager and dresses like one. She could easily attract a man and become infatuated for a while. Karen often picks low-functioning men. Her rationalization is that she can have more control and she hopes they will appreciate her. But Karen picks low-functioning men mainly so that it will be easy for her to devalue them and eventually reject them. When she finds a man who treats her well, she feels less passion, becomes demanding, dependent, provoking fights, and blames the conflicts on the boyfriend.

Karen notices my wheaten terrier, Roy, who remains behind my chair. He is friendly and likes to greet most people.

"Your dog looks depressed. It's no wonder since he has to listen to all this crap."

"Karen, what can I do for you?" I ask. Clearly, it was Karen who feels depressed, projecting her feelings onto my dog. Karen transfers onto me that I will not be able to endure her "crap." She can barely stand her own emotions (poor affect tolerance), so she had a hard time imagining someone as an adequate emotional container. She cannot realize how much she is already showing me about herself.

Looking at me insistently, she demands, "I want you to help me find a man."

"I'm an analyst not a matchmaker," I say, clarifying my role.

"I keep picking jerks," she says, shrugging to suggest her victimhood.

"What do you want?"

"I don't want to be alone . . . I want to be married."

"Not *happily* married?"

She is silent.

Karen is not ready for an interpretation. An interpretation is a translation from unconscious to conscious language. Dreams, slips of the tongue, psychological symptoms, and relationship conflicts are all forms of unconscious language. Interpretation helps a person develop self-reflection. Self-reflection can help a person be more comfortable with themselves and others. Karen wants love to protect her. She wants to be the cared-for child and her man to be an undemanding ideal parent. I could have interpreted that the real reason Karen did not say, "Happily married" is because it isn't consistent with her conflicted attachment style. Her history with men proves this.

From the time I first met Karen, I saw many of the themes to come. I see her problems with attachment by how she treats me (transference).

An interpretation goes into forbidden territory, into a person's most private place. I never go there without an invitation. For now, in this first phase of treatment, I make no deep interpretations; rather I clarify our roles and tasks.

"If you want me to help you to have a healthy intimacy, you must allow yourself to have a therapeutic relationship with me. It will take emotional honesty, time, and commitment."

Karen says, "I don't have the time and money. They don't pay nurses what they should."

Karen feels entitled to happiness. She does not understand that she has to earn it.

"Your time and money will go to other things that will not affect your life as profoundly as psychotherapy."

"Sure. Sure." Karen sneers in a dismissive tone.

An emotionally corrective relationship could help a person have better intimacy. Psychotherapy is the most reliable method. But here is the irony: One needs to have the capacity for intimacy to form a therapeutic relationship to start with. In other words, it takes a good patient to get to the good therapy.

These qualities make for good patients:

1. A commitment to the therapeutic relationship,
2. Openness to constructive feedback,
3. Emotional insight into one's own flaws,
4. A capacity for concern and remorse,
5. A sense of responsibility for one's actions and situation in life, and
6. A willingness to be a better person.

If a patient cannot do these things, there is no deep psychotherapy. There can be no increased ability for self-reflection, self-soothing, affect tolerance, resiliency, and understanding others. There is no increased ability for healthy love.

"Can you help me?" Karen demands.

I am not about to tell Karen at this point that she needs to develop many of the qualities that she so dearly lacks. Instead, I remind her of the protective boundary and ground rules of the therapy. Karen knows them, but like many patients, she will test the limits to see if I am trustworthy and professional. Karen has internal chaos. She brings chaos to her relationships. The structure and limits of the therapy might help her develop more structure and cohesion within her personality.

"I lease a regular time to you out of my practice. You are financially responsible for this leased time. We start on time and end on time. There are strict privacy rules. This firm boundary and commitment will intensify the treatment. I can't help you with intimacy without a therapeutic commitment." As I explain the details of the ground rules, Karen grows impatient.

"I know you have control problems," Karen says.

"If you come regularly and work hard you will probably have improvement."

"How much?"

Research shows that psychotherapy interventions are highly effective. But the main factors that lead to improvement are the personality qualities of the patient and the therapist and their relationship (Wampold, 2001). I need to have a healthy capacity to empathize with my patients. My empathy is often expressed in the tone, timing, and accuracy of the therapeutic interventions. I apply the interventions as paint from a palette. I mix and apply as needed the right amounts of listening, questioning, clarifying, confronting, interpreting, and reconstructions of the psychological past.

Mostly, I am silent when I work, actively listening to my patients. My silence in a safe atmosphere promotes a sense of autonomy and self-reflection in the patient. It also allows me to form a deep understanding of what the patient is trying to unconsciously communicate. (It is hard to show how silence works in writing. In reality, I do a lot of listening that is not evident in this story.) My empathic listening provides a psychological container for the patient's emotions. When patients cannot tolerate their affects, they can be laundered in our bi-personal field. They internalize my reactions and learn to better self-reflect, regulate their affects, and self-soothe.

When an infant fusses, a mothering figure holds, launders, and helps to contain the child's emotions (Bion, 1962). Children internalize this early emotional environment in their implicit unconscious memory. Research has found that a person's capacity for self-reflection, affect regulation, self-soothing, and a core sense of self and others evolves from this early interaction. These infant attachment and brain studies have lead to a reformulation of psychoanalytic treatment. We now believe more than ever that working with affects in an empathic relationship is one of the most important growth factors in psychotherapy (Fonagy, Gergely, Jurist, Target, 2002). If I intervene out of my own discomfort with the patient's emotions and just focus on symptom relief, I am not acting as a good container. Seeing Karen's problems in terms of her symptoms would reinforce her assumption that she is unknowable and that only the surface counts.

I use questions to take a patient deeper into personality. Questions may be used to get more information necessary for an interpretation or a reconstruction. Clarifications help improve reality testing, so that a patient might not continue operating on assumptions that are irrational or false.

When a patient is considering acting out in a destructive manner, there is often no time for an interpretation aimed at developing a more mature personality. I use confrontation to remind the patient of the consequences of acting out.

Interpretations of unconscious transferences, defenses, resistances, and conflicts promote more insight and psychological maturity. Reconstruction of repressed areas of a patient's life helps develop a more cohesive sense of self. Reconstructing a psychological history can help patients make sense out of their symptoms and relationships.

I can never know a patient's true history. But having a sense of a continuous self that was built over time and can continue to grow over time is an important insight. Reconstructions allow a person to master problems that could not have been understood, tolerated, or resolved earlier in life.

Almost everyone can benefit from venting in a supportive atmosphere. Most people find that the therapist's questions, clarifications, confrontations, and even suggestions help them with symptom reduction. But a psychoanalytically informed psychotherapist is specifically trained to use interpretations and reconstructions while acting as a good emotional container so that there is an actual maturation in personality structure.

Freud's goal of psychoanalysis was to achieve a profound growth of the mind so that the person can work and love better. Interpretations and reconstructions of the unconscious self-defeating side of personality are important ingredients in such profound changes.

Unfortunately, interpretations and reconstructions are frequently of limited value with patients who are concrete in their thinking and have little insight. For those individuals, cognitive-behavioral interventions that are symptom focused may be more effective. These interventions are similar to the psychoanalytic interventions of questioning, clarifying, and confronting.

There are few psychotherapists inclined to devote an extra 5 years of postdoctoral work in training and their own psychoanalysis required for a specialization in psychoanalysis. There are few patients willing to put in the time and money for anything more than surface symptom relief. Psychoanalysis would then seem to be a dying art and science. However, with a growing body of neuropsychoanalytic research to support it (Schore, 1994), psychoanalysis has become one of the largest divisions of the American Psychological Association. I have found that with every patient a psychoanalytic formulation is useful in helping me to understand what symptoms mean in the context of the whole person (McWilliams, 1994, 1999).

I understand Karen's off-putting defenses. She is scared. She has an insecure attachment style, probably due to traumas in her childhood (Ainsworth, Blehar, Waters, and Wall, 1978; Bowlby, 1982; McCarthy and Taylor, 1999). Karen feels that it is best to trust no one, pretend to be self-sufficient, and demand intimacy but avoid it.

In the initial stage of treatment (Howard, Moras, Brill, Martinovich, and Lutz, 1996), the first thing to do is to give a patient hope that things can get better. When patients come into treatment, they are often demoralized. When Karen said at the beginning of the session, "Dr. Gordon, I came back to you because I tried everything else," she was telling me how demoralized she was. She does not want a therapeutic relationship with me. She does not believe that anything good could come from a committed intimacy. She thinks that if she stays too long in a relationship, she will be disappointed and hurt. Karen came back only after all else failed. But she wants a magical cure.

The next phase of treatment often is about reducing symptoms, learning new skills and insights. That can happen in a few sessions to a few months. But her problem is not about a lack of skills. It is a deep fear of intimacy that is most likely based on a damaged self and trauma from childhood. However, Karen does not want to go there.

Few patients stay long enough to go into the third phase of psychotherapy, the reconstructive phase of treatment, and have personal growth. It could take years to change personality traits in order for a person to have personal growth and a better capacity for healthy love (Gordon, 2001, and also, Monsen, Odland, Faugli, Daae, et al., 1995). Reconstructive treatment such as that found in psychoanalytic psychotherapy requires the patient to form an intimate alliance with the therapist and to self-reflect. I am concerned that Karen could not do that enough. She is too defensive for it. Karen needs to think that the answers to her problems will come from an idealized rescuer. She is waiting for her messiah.

I say, "How much improvement you make depends on what you put into it. I will need to see you twice a week to start, otherwise we will not get deep enough to change personality traits."

From chapter 26 (section from the Russian lecture) and more developed in my "What Is Love? A Unified Model of Love Relations," in *Issues in Psychoanalytic Psychology* (2006e).

I have not found a single theory to explain the complexity of love relations. I have developed my own integrated meta-theory to help understand why romantic love is so irrational. Imagine a pyramid with species traits, individual traits, relational internalizations, beliefs, and context as five levels (see Figure 12.1).

At the base of the pyramid is the most powerful influence on our behaviors, our *species traits,* which we possess as a result of millions of years of natural selection. They define how we love as a human species (as compared to other animals). What we as humans find attractive in a mate are physical features and emotional triggers that used to

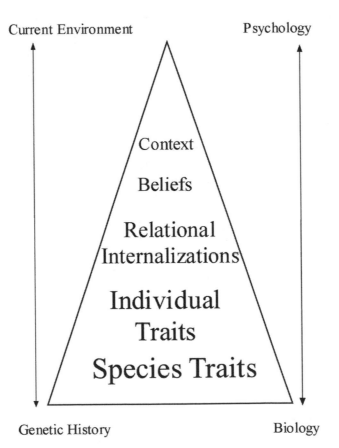

Figure 12.1   An integrated model of factors contributing to love relations.

be associated with survival, protection, and reproductive ability. They helped the species survive for millions of years, but have little to do with the survival of a couple's love today. A woman may be attracted to a powerful man or a man may be attracted to a beautiful woman, but these qualities have nothing to do with the ability to maintain a loving relationship. These instinctual influences weaken as a person matures.

The next level is *individual traits*. Humans are mainly alike in behaviors, but we are all born with different temperaments or traits. Researchers have consistently found, for example, that extraversion, neuroticism, aggressiveness, and impulsivity are largely inherited traits (Ahadi, and Rothbart, 1994; Zuckerman, 2003). People who are too insecure, hostile, or insensitive will have intimacy problems. Good or bad parenting will mitigate or aggravate these negative traits.

Next is the influence of our parents, our earliest attachments, and family dynamics. These *relational internalizations* become part of a person's unconscious personality. An infant's attachment style is likely to be unconsciously repeated in later love relations. A secure attachment to a good enough mothering figure and parents who help a child deal with aggression, sexuality, and provide for a healthy self-concept are just some of the interpersonal prerequisites to loving maturely. Childhood neglect and abuse does damage to personality and the capacity to trust. A person who is naturally resilient may later learn to love maturely with psychotherapy despite an unhappy childhood.

After we look at ourselves as human animals, then as individuals with innate personality traits, and then influenced by parenting, we now look at the period from later childhood into adulthood and the influence of cognitive learning. This next level is our learned *beliefs* from cultural norms and personal romantic experiences. People often think that marrying someone who fits an ideal family or cultural stereotype, or someone the opposite of a toxic parent or last lover is the solution to their mistakes in romantic choices. These beliefs are often superstitious and biased. A relationship is more likely to be successful if the couple shares beliefs that promote altruism, honesty, fairness, and mutual concern.

The top level is the *current psychological context*. The time in a person's life or current stressful circumstances can produce conditions for an overidealization of another. For example, the Stockholm syndrome is a psychological reaction that leads to an attraction to a person holding one captive (Kuleshnyk, 1984). A situation in a person's life can create a need for a certain kind of relationship. Later, when the condition changes, the romance fades. Love that is based on a true appreciation of the other's qualities is likely to last.

As you move up the pyramid you are moving from evolutionary history to current psychological context. All these combined levels contribute to the irrationality of romantic love. The most disturbed relationships are based more on instinctual triggers, with individuals with immature personality traits, on toxic internalizations and attachment traumas, on irrational beliefs about love objects, and on a current stressful context that distorts the value of another.

# In Conclusion

What can I share with you from my study of love, intimacy, and personal growth as a scientist-practitioner?

My understanding of love started with love as an exchangeable interpersonal resource. Love brings happiness, but also pain. Falling in love is instinctual. It is an overidealization of another in service to reproduction for the survival of the species. We are genetically programmed to have a sex drive and to find a desirable mate.

However, our genes did not program us to remain in love. We need concern and tenderness for that. Concern and tenderness are dependent on a person's emotional maturity, which results from a normal temperament and having had good enough parenting. A person who has a normal temperament and had good enough parents is likely to have rewarding intimacy.

Typically, after a period of idealization of the beloved, tensions in the relationship mount. If emotional maturity does not take over what passion started, the relationship will wither in time. A person with an immature personality will have disturbed love relations due to their high degree of defensiveness, egocentricity, and aggression.

I developed a comprehensive model of love relations by integrating evolutionary psychology, object relations, and cognitive and social psychology. This theoretical model lets us see why love can be so irrational. Love relations are based in primitive instincts. They are subject to problems in temperament. They are subject to problems from the child–parent relationship. They are subject to cultural biases and expectations. They are subject to situational stresses. Love is attacked from all angles.

We regress in intimacy. Old hurts and emotions emerge. Love relations are an opportunity to unconsciously repeat the past or grow from it. We can all learn to love better with personal growth. Personal growth takes time and hard work. We earn it with commitment, openness to constructive feedback, emotional insight into one's own flaws, a capacity for concern and remorse, a sense of responsibility for one's actions and situation in life, and a willingness to be a better person. Psychoanalytic psychotherapy can reach a deep enough level for personal growth.

After 30 years of thinking about love, intimacy, and personal growth, I have gone from a circumplex to a pyramid. However, one thing remains true. We are richer for being loving. It is worth the effort to learn how to love better.

# Index

intimacy requirement, 111
Parental Alienation Syndrome pa-
    tients, 48–49
transference/countertransference,
    24–25, 27–32
unconscious dynamics, 27
therapists
    fees, 25
    gifts from patients, 32
    professional maturity, 87
    psychoanalysis for, 28–29
    theoretical orientation, 87, 89, 100
thoughts, 64
traits, 19–22, 116–117. *See also*
    MMPI/MMPI-2 (Minnesota
    Multiphasic Personality
    Inventory)
transference, 24–25, 27–32
trauma, 89, 97, 98
Treboux, D., 105
Troll, L., 37

"true self," 15, 99
trust, 117

**U**

unconscious, 7, 26, 27, 94, 110

**V**

Veron, E., 12
von Rad, M., 66–67

**W**

Wallerstein, Judith S., 38, 104–106
Wallwork, E., 26–27
Waters, E., 105
Weiner, I. B., 67
Welsh, G. S., 20
Westen, D., 66
Winnicott, D. W., 15, 32
Wolberg, Lewis, 7
women, 37, 38. *See also* mothers

# References

Ainsworth, M. D., Blehar, M., Waters, E., & Wall, S. (1978). *Patterns of attachment*. Hillsdale, NJ: Erlbaum.

Ahadi, S. S., & Rothbart, M. K. (1994). Temperament, development and the big five. In R. M. C. Halverson, & G. Kohnstanamm (Eds.) *The developing structure of temperament and personality from infancy to adulthood* (pp. 189–208). Hillsdale, NJ: Erhbaum.

Akhtar, S. (1999). *Inner torment—Living between conflict and fragmentation*. New York, London: Jason Aronson, Inc.

Beck, A. T., Ward, C. H., Mendelsohn, M., Mock, J. E., & Erbaugh, J. K. (1961). An inventory for measuring depression. *Archives of General Psychology, 4,* 561–571.

Biller, H. B. (1971). Fathering and female sexual development. *Medical Aspects of Human Sexuality, 5*(11), 126–138.

Bion, W. R. (1962). *Learning from experience:* London: Heinemann.

Bowlby, J. (1982). *Attachment and loss*. New York: Jason Aronson.

Dahlstrom, W. G., Welsh, G. S., & Dahlstrom, L. E. (1972). *An MMPI handbook: I. Clinical interpretation.* (Rev. ed.), (pp. xxvi, 507). Oxford, England: University of Minnesota Press.

Dunne, J., & Hedrick, M. (1994). The parent alienation syndrome: An analysis of sixteen selected cases. *Journal of Divorce & Remarriage, 21*(3–4), 21–38.

Fairbairn, W. R. D. (1952). *An object relations theory of personality*. New York: Basic Books.

Fenchel, G. H. (1998). *The mother–daughter relationship echoes through time*. Northvalw, NJ: Jason Aronson, Inc.

Fiske, D. W. (1957). The constraints on intraindividual variability in test responses. *Educational and Psychological Measurement, 17,* 317-337.

Foa, U. G., & Foa, E. B. (1974). *Societal structures of the mind*. Springfield, IL: Charles C. Thomas.

Fonagy, P., Gergely, G. Jurist, E. L. & Target, M. (2002). *Affect regulation, Mentalization and the development of the self*. New York: Other Press.

Framo, J. L. (1976.). Family of origin as a therapeutic resource for adults in marital and family therapy: You can and should go home again. *Family Process,15*(2), 193–209.

Frank, F.D., Lindley, B.S., & Cohen, R.A. (1981, July). *Standards for Psychological*

*Assessment of Nuclear Facility Personnel*. NUREG/CR-2075. Washington, DC: U.S. Nuclear Regulatory Commission.

Freud, S. (1913). On beginning the treatment (Further recommendations on the technique of psycho-analysis I). In *The standard edition of the complete psychological works of Sigmund Freud, Volume XII (1911–1913): The case of Schreber, papers on technique and other works* (pp. 121–144), New York, N.Y., W. W. Norton & Company.

Freud, S. (1915). Observations on transference — love (Further recommendations on the technique of psycho-analysis III). In *The standard edition of the complete psychological works of Sigmund Freud, Volume XII (1911–1913): The case of Schreber, papers on technique and other works* (pp. 157–171) New York, N.Y., W. W. Norton & Company.

Gardner, R. A. (1987). *The parental alienation syndrome and the differentiation between fabricated and genuine child abuse*. Cresskill, NJ: Creative Therapeutics.

Gardner, R. A. (2002a). Denial of the parental alienation syndrome also harms women. *American Journal of Family Therapy, 30*,3, 191–202.

Gardner, R. A. (2002b). Parental alienation syndrome vs. parental alienation: Which diagnosis should evaluators use in child-custody disputes? *American Journal of Family Therapy, 30*(2), 93–115.

Gilroy, P. J., Carroll, L., & Murra, J. (2002). A preliminary survey of counseling psychologists' personal experiences with depression and treatment, *Professional Psychology: Research and Practice, 33*, 402–407.

Graham, J. R. (2000). *MMPI-2 Assessing personality and psychopathology*. New York: Oxford University Press, Inc.

Graham, J. R., Ben-Porath, Y. S., & McNutly, J. L. (1999). *MMPI-2 Correlates for outpatient community mental health settings*. Minneapolis: University of Minnesota Press.

Guntrip, H. (1969). *Schizoid phenomena, object relations and the self*. New York: International Universities Press.

Hathaway, S. R., & McKinley, J. C. (1942). A multiphasic personality schedule (Minnesota): III. The measurement of symptomatic depression. *Journal of Psychology, 14,* 73–84.

Hetherington, M. E., & Stanley, M. (1999). The adjustment of children with divorced parents: A risk and resiliency perspective. *Journal of Child Psychology & Psychiatry, 40*(1), 129–140.

Hollon, S., & Mandell, M. (1979). Use of the MMPI in the evaluation of treatment effects. In J. E. Butcher (Ed.), *New Developments in the use of the MMPI* (pp. 241–302). Minneapolis: University of Minnesota Press.

Horn, J. (1976). Love: The most important ingredient in happiness [summary of dissertation by R. M. Gordon]. *Psychology Today, 10* (2), 98–102.

Howard, K. I., Moras, K., Brill, P. L., Martinovich, Z., & Lutz, W. (1996). Evaluation of psychotherapy. Efficacy, effectiveness, and patient progress. *American Psychologist, 51*(10), 1059–1064.

Jacobs, J. W. (1988). Euripides' Medea: A psychodynamic model of severe divorce pathology. *American Journal of Psychotherapy, 42*(2), 308–319.

Jackson, D. (1964). *Myths of Madness: New Facts for Old Fallacies*. NY, MacMillian Pub. Co.

Juni, S. & Grimm, D. W. (1993). Sex-role similarities between adults and their parents. *Contemporary Family Therapy, 15*(3), 247–251.

Kelly, J. B. (1993). Current research on children's postdivorce adjustment: No simple answers. *Family & Conciliation Courts Review, 31*(1) 29–49.

Kelly, J. B., and Johnston, J. R. (2001). The alienated child: A reformulation of parental alienation syndrome. *Family Court Review, 39*(3), 249–266.

Kernberg, O. F. (1976). *Object-relations theory and clinical psychoanalysis*. New York: Jason Aronson.

Kernberg, O. F. (1980). *Internal world and external reality: Object relations theory applied*. New York: Jason Aronson.

Kernberg, O. F. (1989). *Psychodynamic psychotherapy of borderline patients*. New York: Basic Books.

Kernberg, O. F. (1995). *Love relations: Normality and pathology*. New Haven, CT: Yale University Press.

Kordy, H., von Rad, M., & Senf, W. (1989). Empirical hypotheses on the psychotherapeutic treatment of psychosomatic patients in short and long-term time-unlimited psychotherapy. *Psychotherapy and Psychosomatics, 52*(1–3), 155–163.

Kramer, S. (1995). Parents' hatred of their children: An understudied aspect of cross-generational aggression. In S. Akhtar, S. Kramer, & H. Parens (Eds.), *The birth of hatred* (pp. 3–14). Northvale, N.J: Jason Aronson, Inc.

Kuleshnyk, I. (1984). The Stockholm syndrome: Toward an understanding. *Social Action and the Law, 10*(2), 37–42.

Lana, R. E. (1991). *Assumptions of social psychology: A reexamination.* Hillside, NJ: Lawrence Erlbaum Associates.

Leon, G. R., Gillum, B., Gillum, R., & Gouze, M. (1979). Personality stability and change over a 30-year period—middle age to old age. *Journal of Consulting and Clinical Psychology, 47*(3), 517–524.

Luborsky, L. (1984). *Principles of psychoanalytic psychotherapy: A manual for supportive-expressive treatment.* New York: Basic Books.

McCarthy, G. & Taylor, A. (1999). Avoidant/ambivalent attachment style as a mediator between abusive childhood experiences and adult relationship difficulties. *Journal of Child Psychology and Psychiatry and Allied Disciplines, 40*(3), 465–477.

McWilliams, N. (1994). *Psychoanalytic diagnosis understanding personality structure in the clinical process.* New York: Guilford Press.

McWilliams, N. (1999). *Psychoanalytic case formulation.* New York: Guilford Press.

Monsen, J., Odland, T., Faugli, A., Daae, E., et al. (1995). Personality disorders and psychosocial changes after intensive psychotherapy: A prospective follow-up of an outpatient psychotherapy project, 5 years after end of treatment. *Scandinavian Journal of Psychology, 36*(3), 256–268.

O'Donohue, W., Buchanan, J. A., & Fisher, J. E. (2000). Characteristics of empirically supported treatments. *Journal of Psychotherapy Practice and Research, 9*(2), 69–74.

Olver, R. R. Aries, E., & Batgos, J. (1989). Self-other differentiation and the mother-child relationship: The effects of sex and birth order. *Journal of Genetic Psychology, 150*(3), 311–322.

Otto, R. K. & Collins, R. (1995). Use of the MMPI-2/MMPI-A in child custody evaluations. In J. G. Y. Ben-Porath, G.C.N. Hall & M. Zaragoza (Eds.), *Forensic applications of the MMPI-2*. Newbury Park, CA: Sage Publications.

Panksepp, J. (1998). *Affective neuroscience: The foundations of human and animal emotions* (pp. xii, 466). New York: Oxford University Press.

Panksepp, J. (2004). Basic affects and the instinctual emotional systems of the brain: The primordial sources of sadness, joy, and seeking. In A. S. R. Manstead, N. Frijda, & A. Fischer (Eds.), *Feelings and emotions: The Amsterdam symposium* (pp. 174–193). New York: Cambridge University Press.

Pope, K., & Tabachnick, B. G. (1994). Therapists as patients: A national survey of psychologists' experiences, problems, and beliefs. *Professional Psychology: Research & Practice, 25*(3), 247–258.

Pine, F. (1995). On the origin and evolution of a species of hate: A clinical-literary excursion. In S. Akhtar, S. Kramer, H. Parens, (Eds.), *The birth of hatred. Developmental, clinical, and technical aspects of intense aggression* (pp. 105–132). Northvale, NJ and London: Jason Aronson, Inc.

Schore, A. N. (1994). *Affect regulation and the origin of the self. The neurobiology of emotional development:* Hillside, NJ: Lawrence Erlbaum Associates.

Seligman, M. E. (1996). Science as an ally of practice. *American Psychologist, 51*(10), 1072–1079.

Sluzki, C. E., Beavin, J., Tanopolsky, A., & Veron, E. (1967). Transactional disqualification. Research on the double bind. *Archives of General Psychiatry, 16,* 494–504.

Smith, M. L., & Glass, G. V. (1979). Meta-analysis of psychotherapy outcome studies. In C. A. Kiesler, N. A. Cummings & G. R. VandenBos (Eds.), *Psychology and national health insurance: A sourcebook.* (pp. 530–539). Washington, DC: American Psychological Association.

Spiro III, A., Butcher, J. N., Levenson, R. M., Aldwin, C. M., & Bosse, R. (2000). Change and stability in personality: A five-year study of the MMPI-2 in older men. In J. E. Butcher (Ed.), *Basic sources on the MMPI-2* (pp. 443–462). Minneapolis: University of Minnesota Press.

Steele, B. F. (1970) Parental abuse of infants and small children In: Parenthood: Its Psychology and Psychopathology E. J. Anthony and T. Benedek (eds.). Boston: Little, Brown and Company, pp. 449-477.

Stevens, S. E., Hynan, M. T., & Allen, M. (2000, fall). A meta-analysis of common factor and specific treatment effects across the outcome domains of the phase model of psychotherapy. *Clinical psychology: Science and practice,* 273–290.

Stierlin, H. (1970). The function of inner objects. *International Journal of Psychoanalysis, 51,* 321–329. *666.*

Subotnik, L. (1972). Spontaneous remission of deviant MMPI profiles among college students. *Journal of Consulting and Clinical Psychology, 38*(2), 191–201.

Swenson, W. M., Pearson, J. S., & Osborne, D. (1973). *An MMPI source book. Basic item, scale, and pattern data on 50,000 medical patients.* Minneapolis: University of Minnesota Press.

Troll, L. (1987). Mother-daughter relationship through the life span. *Applied Social Psychology Annual, 7,* 284–305.

Wallerstein, J.S. & Corbin, S.B. (1989). Daughters of divorce: Report from a ten-year follow-up. *American Journal of Orthopsychiatry,* *59*(4) 593–604.

Wallerstein, J. S., & Lewis, J. M. (2004). The unexpected legacy of divorce: Report of a 25-year study. *Psychoanalytic Psychology,* *21*(3), 353–370.

Wallerstein, J. S., & Lewis, J. M. (2005). The reality of divorce. Reply to Gordon (2005). *Psychoanalytic Psychology,* 22(3), 452–454.

Wallwork, E. (1991). *Psychoanalysis and ethics* (pp. xiii, 344). New Haven, CT: Yale University Press.

Walters, E., Merrick, S., Treboux, D., Crowell, J. & Albersheim, L. (2000). Attachment security in infancy and early adulthood: A twenty-year longitudinal study. *Child Development, 71*(3), 684–689.

Wampold, B. E. (2001). *The great psychotherapy debate: Models, methods, and findings.* Mahwah, NJ: Lawrence Erlbaum.

Weiner, I. B., & Exner, J. E., Jr. (1991). Rorschach changes in long-term and short-term psychotherapy. *Journal of Personality Assessment,* *56*(3), 453–465.

Westen, D. (2000). The efficacy of dialectical behavior therapy for borderline personality disorder. *Clinical Psychology: Science and Practice, 7,* 92–94.

Willi, J. (1982). *Couples in collusion.* New York: Jason Aronson.

Winnicott, D. W. (1955.). *Metapsychological and clinical aspects of regression within the psychoanalytical set up.* In *Collected Papers.* London: Tavistock; New York: Basic Books.

Winnicott, D. W. (1965). *The family and individual development* (pp. viii, 181). Oxford, England: Basic Books.

Zuckerman, M. (2003). Biological bases of personality. In T. Millon & M. J. Lerner (Eds.), *Handbook of psychology: Personality and social psychology, Vol. 5.* (pp. 85–116). New York: John Wiley & Sons.

## Publications of Robert M. Gordon

(Publications are in descending date order; some include coauthors. Many can be viewed as full articles at: www.mmpi-info.com)

Gordon, R. M., Stoffey, R., & Bottinelli, J. (in press, 2008). MMPI-2 findings of primitive defenses in alienating parents. *American Journal of Family Therapy.*

Gordon, R. M. (2007a). To wit or not to wit: The use of humor in psychotherapy. *Pennsylvania Psychologist, 67*(3), 22–24.

Gordon, R. M. (2007b). *I love you madly! Workbook: Insight enhancement about healthy and disturbed love relations.* Allentown, PA: IAPT Press.

Gordon, R. M. (2007c, spring). The powerful combination of the MMPI-2 and the *Psychodynamic Diagnostic Manual, Independent Practitioner,* 84–85.

Gordon, R. M. (2007d, November/December). PDM valuable in identifying high-risk patients *National Psychologist, 16,* (6), November/ December, page 4.

Gordon, R. M. (2006e). What is love? A unified model of love relations, *Issues in Psychoanalytic Psychology, 28*(1), 25–33.

Moyer, D. M., Gordon, R. M., Ward, J. T., & Burkhardt, B. B. (2006f). Characteristics of successful fakers versus unsuccessful fakers: Is empathy, intelligence, or personality associated with faking PTSD on the MMPI-2? *Psychological Reports, 99,* 747–750.

Gordon, R. M. (2006g). Psychoanalytic reflections on love and Sexuality: Book review. *Issues in Psychoanalytic Psychology, 28*(2), 85–89.

Gordon, R. M. (2006a). The APA Ethics Code as a projective test. *Psychologist-Psychoanalyst XXVI*(1), 67–68.

Gordon, R. M. (2006b). *I love you madly! On passion, personality and personal growth*. Charleston SC: Booksurge.

Gordon, R.M. (2006c). False assumptions about psychopathology, hysteria and the MMPI-2 restructured clinical scales. *Psychological Reports, 98*, 870–872.

Gordon, R.M. (2006d). *An expert look at love, intimacy and personal growth*. (First Edition), Allentown, PA: IAPT Press.

Gordon, R. M. (2005a). The doom and gloom of divorce research: Comment on Wallerstein and Lewis (2004). *Psychoanalytic Psychology, 22*(3), 450–451.

Gordon, R. M. (2005b, September) The ethics of supervising a family member. *Pennsylvania Psychologist, 5*–6.

Gordon, R. M. (2005c, June 28). Judge psychology by results and scientific studies. *Morning Call* (Allentown, Pennsylvania).

Gordon, R M. (2003a, January). Towards a theoretically individuated and integrated family therapist. *Psychotherapy* (Moscow), *1*, 18–24 (In Russian).

Gordon, R. M. (2003b, July). The countertransference controversy. *Pennsylvania Psychologist, 8*–9

Moyer, D., Burkhardt, B., & Gordon, R. M. (2002). Faking PTSD from a motor vehicle accident on the MMPI-2. *American Journal of Forensic Psychology, 20*(2), 747-750.

Gordon, R. M. (2002). *Child custody evaluators: Psychologists or detectives?* Mechanicsburg, PA: Pennsylvania Bar Institute.

Gordon, R. M. (2001). MMPI/MMPI-2 changes in long-term psychoanalytic psychotherapy. *Issues in Psychoanalytic Psychology, 23*(1–2), 59–79.

Gordon, R. M. (2000, June). Boundary: Protection, limits and safety. *Pennsylvania Psychologist,* 4-5.

Gordon, R. M. (1999, July 23). Recovering Bodies A Crucial Part In Grieving, Dealing With Death *Morning Call,* A-11, Allentown, PA.

Gordon, R. M. (1998). The Medea Complex and the parental alienation syndrome: When mothers damage their daughter's ability to love a man. In Gerd H. Fenchel (Ed.), *The mother–daughter relationship echoes through time.* Northvale, NJ: Jason Aronson, Inc.

Gordon, R. M. (1997, February). Handling transference and countertransference issues with the difficult patient. *Pennsylvania Psychologist Quarterly,* 20,24. Also reprinted in *Independent Practitioner* (summer 1998), *18*(3), 147–149.

Gordon, R. M. (1995a, fall). Common mistakes made with the MMPI, MMPI-2 and MMPI-A, *Hawaii Psychologist,* 11–12.

Gordon, R. M. (1995b). The symbolic nature of the supervisory relationship: Identification and professional growth, *Issues in Psychoanalytic Psychology, 17*(2), 154–162.

Gordon, R. M. (1993). Ethics based on protection of the transference. *Issues in Psychoanalytic Psychology, 15*(2), 95–105.

Gordon, R. M. (1990a). A job selection interview form for screening secure positions. In Peter Keller & Steven Heyman (Eds.), *Innovations in clinical practice: A source book* (pp. 275–285). Sarasota, FL: Professional Resource Exchange, Inc.

Gordon, R. M. (1990b, December). Changing your MMPI booklet to incorporate some of the advantages of the MMPI-2, *Pennsylvania Psychologist.*

Gordon, R. M. (1989a, November). Is it really better? *Pennsylvania Psychologist.*

Gordon, R. M. (1989b). *Interpreting MMPI subtle scales as representing defense mechanisms.* Paper presented at the 24th Annual Symposium on Recent Developments in the Use of the MMPI, Hawaii.

Gordon, R. M. (1987a). Suggestions on the use of the MMPI in child custody evaluations: Case examples of detecting paranoia in false negative profiles. The 10th International Conference on Personality Assessment: Brussels, Belgium.

Gordon, R. M. (1987b). Interpreting Weiner's obvious and subtle scales in terms of the psychodynamics of conflict and defense. The 10th International Conference on Personality Assessment: Brussels, Belgium.

Bennett Woolever, Debra Kay & Gordon, R. M. (1986, October). How to pick a good apple. *Security Management,* 101–103.

Gordon, R. M. (1984a). *The MMPI psychotherapist's psychodiagnostic report 400/566.* Allentown, PA: International Information Systems.

Gordon, R. M. (1984b). *The MMPI-168 psychotherapist's report.* Allentown, PA: International Information Systems.

Gordon, R. M. (1984c). *The MMPI personnel report 168, 400/566.* Allentown, PA: International Information Systems.

Gordon, R. M. (1984d). *The MMPI Security Report 168, 400/566.* Allentown, PA: International Information Systems.

Gordon, R. M. (1984e). *The MMPI physician's psychodiagnostic report 168, 400/566.* Allentown, PA: International Information Systems.

Gordon, R. M. (1982). Systems-object relations view of marital therapy: Revenge and reraising. In L. R. Wolberg, & M. Aronson, *Group and Family Therapy,* 325–333, New York: M., Brunner-Mazel.

Gordon, R. M. (1980). A concurrent validity study of the CAQ and MMPI. In Samuel E. Krug (Ed.), *Clinical analysis manual,* (pp. 17–20). Savoy, IL: Institute for Personality and Ability Testing.

Gordon, R. M. (1978). Imprecision or dissonance? A reply to Harris and Harvey. *Journal of Consulting and Clinical Psychology, 46,* 329–330.

Gordon, R. M. (1976). Effects of volunteering and responsibility on the perceived value and effectiveness of a clinical treatment. *Journal of Consulting and Clinical Psychology, 44,* 799–801.

Gordon, R. M. (1975). Effects of interpersonal and economic resources upon values and the quality of life. *Dissertation Abstracts International, 36,* 3122B. (University Microfilms No. 75–28, 220).

Weissman, H. N., Goldschmid, M. L., Gordon, R. M., & Feinberg, H. (1972). Changes in self-regard, creativity, and interpersonal behavior as a function of audio-tape encounter groups. *Psychological Reports, 31,* 975–981.

Shure, M. B., Spivak, G., & Gordon, R. M. (1972, May). Problem-solving thinking: A preventive mental health program for pre-school children. *Reading World, II*(4) 259-273.

Weissman, H. N., Ritter, K., & Gordon, R. M. (1971). Reliability study of the defense mechanism inventory. *Psychological Reports, 24,* 1237–1238.

# Continuing Education (CE)

## Psychologists Can Earn 10 CE Credits

The Institute for Advanced Psychological Training is an organization approved by the American Psychological Association to offer continuing education for psychologists. The Institute for Advanced Psychological Training maintains responsibility for the program.

Educational Objectives: Learn: What is love? How do we treat love disturbances? How do we get personal growth? How does psychology study human problems?

This home study course is for any psychologist wishing to learn about healthy and unhealthy relations as a reference for research or for therapeutic work with patients.

We do not offer refunds after the purchase of this book and CE credit. We will give you a CE certificate upon a 70% or better score. You may take the CE exam as often as you wish until you achieve at least a passing score.

Go to www.mmpi-info.com and then to Continuing Education.

## CE Test: Answer true or false.

1. Love is the most particularistic resource on Foa's circumplex.
2. The value of goods increased with less love income.
3. Love brought happiness more than any other resource.
4. A systems view of families helps us understand the unconscious mind.

5. Object relations theory and systems theory are isomorphically linked in a continuous system of inner and outer worlds.
6. The MMPI is not useful in screening for psychopathology.
7. Ethics in psychotherapy is a courtesy, and is not related to treatment outcome.
8. Parental Alienation Syndrome is often the result of a parent with primitive defenses.
9. Depression can result from unresolved losses.
10. The MMPI-2 is not reactive to short-term treatments.
11. Psychoanalytic psychotherapy is strong enough to produce maturation in personality.
12. Since lying is so hard to detect, the psychologist may need to do detective work.
13. Psychotherapists should pick a theory and remain with it.
14. Self-esteem is important to loving others.
15. Gordon believes that children of divorced parents have problems in later relationships because of the divorce.
16. Love relations are dependent on our species traits, individual traits, relational internalization, beliefs from culture, and current emotional context.